Attracting Birds
in the Carolinas

James F. Parnell   William C. Alexander   Frances B. Parnell

Attracting Birds
in the Carolinas

Creating Bird-Friendly Habitats

from the Mountains to the Coast

The University of North Carolina Press

Chapel Hill

Publication of this book was supported in part by
a generous gift from Vicki and Porter Durham.

All photographs in this book
were taken by the authors.

Cover illustrations:
(front) a Red-eyed Vireo
eating a beautyberry,
(back) a female American
Redstart at a birdbath
with a drip fountain.

Designed by Jamison Cockerham
Set in Scala, Scala Sans, Neue Kabel, and Voltage
by Tseng Information Systems, Inc.

Manufactured in the United States of America

The University of North Carolina Press has been a
member of the Green Press Initiative since 2003.

LIBRARY OF CONGRESS CATALOGING-IN-PUBLICATION DATA
Names: Parnell, James F., author. | Alexander, William C.,
   1945– author. | Parnell, Frances Baynor, author.
Title: Attracting birds in the Carolinas : creating bird-friendly
   habitats from the mountains to the coast /
   James F. Parnell, William C. Alexander, Frances B. Parnell.
Description: Chapel Hill : The University of North Carolina
   Press, 2021. | Includes bibliographical references and index.
Identifiers: LCCN 2020026513 | ISBN 9781469662251
   (pbk. : alk. paper) | ISBN 9781469662268 (ebook)
Subjects: LCSH: Bird attracting—North Carolina. | Bird attracting—
   South Carolina. | Birds—North Carolina—Handbooks, manuals,
   etc. | Birds—South Carolina—Handbooks, manuals, etc.
Classification: LCC QL676.56.N67 P37 2021 |
   DDC 598.072/3409756—dc23
LC record available at https://lccn.loc.gov/2020026513

THIS BOOK IS DEDICATED to all the folks in the Carolinas
who share their living spaces, large or small, with our birds. As the
world becomes more crowded with people and as we continue to
eliminate or modify natural habitats to accommodate more people,
we put additional strain on wildlife. It is becoming increasingly
important that we work harder to attract and include birds in
our living spaces. We have a rich history of attracting birds in
the Carolinas, but we need to expand our efforts in the future
if we are to continue to enjoy our wealth of native birdlife.

Contents

Attracting Birds
in the Carolinas

Introduction

People were attracting birds in the Carolinas before the first European settlers arrived. Native Americans erected poles with hanging gourds as nesting sites for Purple Martins, and early European settlers adopted the practice. Many today still consider gourds to be the best nest sites for martins, although large, complex houses are also used. Most Purple Martins nesting in the Carolinas now use some type of artificial nesting structure.

Since those early days, attracting birds—whether intentionally or unintentionally—has taken many forms in the Carolinas. Public and private land management agencies devote large tracts of land to creating appropriate habitats to attract birds. Farmers devote portions of their farms to actively attracting birds or may draw large numbers of birds that feed on waste grain or fruit and berry crops. Homeowners create backyard bird habitats, erect birdhouses, and maintain a variety of feeders. Even apartment dwellers may maintain bird feeders on windowsills or decks.

Agriculture and Development

It is likely that early settlers unintentionally attracted birds through their activities, in much the same way that we do now. Clearing land would have drawn a different group of birds from those living in the forested habitats that existed at the time of settlement. The planting of crops and fruit trees would have enticed many bird species to farms and yards. Cavities in wooden fence posts might well have provided the first artificial nest boxes for Eastern Bluebirds, Brown-headed Nuthatches, and Carolina Chickadees.

Not all early stories of attracting birds are positive. Many bird species are attracted to the grains and fruit in fields and orchards, and with the advent of rice culture in the Low Country of South Carolina and, to some extent, in North Carolina, stories of birds damaging or destroying the rice crop began to appear. The Bobolink, known in earlier times as the rice bird, migrating southward in autumn from nesting areas to the north of the Carolinas, arrived in coastal Carolina when rice was maturing and is recorded as doing great damage to the rice crop. Bobolinks still migrate through the Carolinas in spring and fall, but the rice fields are gone, and the birds are no longer considered a threat. The rice fields probably also attracted waterfowl, which may have been part of early settlers' diet.

A male Purple Martin on a gourd

The Carolina Parakeet also damaged fruit and grain crops in the
Carolinas in colonial times and was considered an important pest by
farmers. The species was last positively recorded in the early 1900s and
was likely extinct by the 1920s, although there were unconfirmed sight-
ings in the Santee River swamps in the 1930s.

Agriculture is still an important business in the Carolinas, and agricultural practices are a major attractant for birds. Grains such as corn,
soybeans, and wheat are major crops and are important to many species
of birds. Birds drawn to newly planted cornfields, sunflower fields, and
fruit and berry orchards still do some damage.

There's also a much more positive connection between birds and
agriculture: birds' gleaning of waste grain in late summer, autumn, and
winter. Modern mechanical harvesting methods still leave waste grain
in the fields at harvesttime, and birds such as Mourning Doves, Canada
Geese, Wild Turkeys, Red-winged Blackbirds, and others feed on this
waste grain. Insect-eating species may also flock to fields at harvesttime
to feed on insects made more vulnerable by the removal of plant cover.

These abundant food sources sometimes come with problems for
the birds. In addition to being perhaps more susceptible to predation in
the very open environment of a field, they may also be exposed to haz-
ardous pesticide and insecticide residues. It also makes sense that any
practice that reduces the insect population in an area will likely also reduce the number of insect-eating birds.

The large lakes in the Carolinas that were created primarily to store
water and to provide a source of energy for hydroelectric power have also

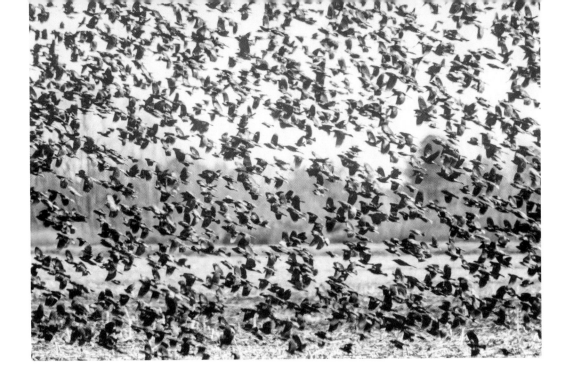

become important attractants for birds. The Santee Cooper project in the 1930s in South Carolina created Lakes Marion and Moultrie, which, in addition to providing water to create electricity, are major draws for both waterfowl and fish-eating birds. Similar lakes, such as Lake Norman and Lake Murray, have caused major changes in the distribution of both waterfowl and fish-eating birds. These large lakes also have had a negative effect on other bird populations because both forests and fields were flooded when they were created, destroying much terrestrial habitat used by birds.

Red-winged Blackbirds in a recently harvested cornfield

Refuges, Sanctuaries, and Other Protected Lands

Wildlife refuges and bird sanctuaries play an important role in both protecting and providing for birds. The first official wildlife refuge in the United States was created in California circa 1870, but it is likely that individual landowners had already declared parts or all of their lands as refuges where the wildlife was protected. In 1903 the first national wildlife refuge, on Pelican Island in Florida, came into being. The first refuge in South Carolina was the Savannah National Wildlife Refuge, established in 1927. It was followed in 1932 by the Cape Romain National Wildlife Refuge. The newest of the eight refuges in South Carolina is the Waccamaw National Wildlife Refuge, established in 1997. The first national wildlife refuge in North Carolina was the Swanquarter National Wildlife Refuge, created in 1932. It was followed in 1934 by the Mattamuskeet National Wildlife Refuge. The newest of the ten North Carolina

A Cooper's Hawk hunting over a marsh

national wildlife refuges is the Pocosin Lakes National Wildlife Refuge, established in 1990. Most of these refuges were created to protect winter habitat and provide food for migrating waterfowl, and they continue to attract large numbers of ducks and geese, as well as other wildlife. In addition, in North Carolina, the Wildlife Resources Commission manages over 2 million acres of public and private lands for wildlife, including birds.

On top of state and federal refuges, there are a number of refuges managed by private individuals or organizations. One interesting private effort to attract birds was Gaddy's Wild Goose Refuge, near Ansonville, North Carolina. Farmer and former hunter Lockhart Gaddy created the refuge in 1934 when he used four tame geese to attract nine Canada Geese to a one-acre pond. Gaddy's Goose Pond, as it was commonly known, grew to attract over 10,000 geese and 1,000 ducks each winter, until it closed in 1975. Presently the Pee Dee National Wildlife Refuge is located only a few hundred yards from the original site of Gaddy's refuge.

A Royal Tern nesting colony on Cape Fear River

Perhaps the most significant effort by a private organization to establish protected areas for birds is the National Audubon Society's creation of a series of sanctuaries in both Carolinas. Audubon came to North Carolina in the early 1900s when it hired wardens to protect colonial waterbird nesting sites in Pamlico Sound, and in the 1980s Audubon established the North Carolina Coastal Islands Sanctuary Program to protect important waterbird nesting islands. That program, which started with two islands in the lower Cape Fear River, now includes nineteen islands from the Cape Fear River north to Ocracoke. In South Carolina, Audubon has established six habitat conservation areas where the protection and enhancement of bird habitats is the primary focus. The Audubon Center and Sanctuary at Francis Beidler Forest and the Silver Bluff Audubon Center and Sanctuary are perhaps the best known of these.

In addition to lands specifically established and managed for wildlife, there are many wilderness areas that are managed in ways that enhance bird habitats. In the Carolinas there are six national forests, encompassing over 1.75 million acres of land. There are also five national parks in the Carolinas and more than eighty state parks in the two states. All protect important bird habitats, and many place birdhouses and bird feeders in portions of the parks. There are also five state forests in the Carolinas and a variety of other entities that protect land for wildlife, including birds.

A male Golden-
winged Warbler
on territory

For many years, certain towns and cities in the Carolinas have been designated bird sanctuaries. Both state legislatures have enacted laws allowing municipalities and other entities to declare themselves bird sanctuaries (see the appendix for details).

Laws and Programs

Legislation has also sought to protect birds themselves, not just their habitats. The Migratory Bird Treaty Act between the United States and Canada was first signed into law in 1918. This law has been amended several times and is a major factor in the protection of migratory birds. It makes it "illegal to take, possess, import, export, transport, sell, purchase, barter, or offer for sale, purchase, or barter, any migratory bird, or the parts, nests, or eggs of such a bird except under the terms of a valid federal permit."

In more recent years, a number of public and private programs have been established to aid birds. The U.S. Fish and Wildlife Service's Urban Bird Treaty program was initiated in 1999 to protect and enhance urban/suburban habitats for birds. It also encourages educating the public about the value of native birds and promotes the management of invasive bird species. In 1973 the National Wildlife Federation started the Backyard Wildlife Habitat program, which is now known as Garden for Wildlife. This program urges people to turn their yard into suitable habitat for wildlife, including pollinators, songbirds, and small mammals. It

A foraging
Red-cockaded
Woodpecker

encourages homeowners to create a healthy habitat for birds by providing food, clean water, and cover (using native plants), and by limiting the use of harmful chemicals.

Recently, the National Audubon Society created the Bird-Friendly Communities program to encourage communities to enhance habitats for birds. This program emphasizes using native plants in landscaping and providing good homes for birds in the form of birdhouses and nest platforms. Reducing the amount of light at night may also cut back on light pollution's disorienting effects on birds, especially during migration. Audubon states that all the participating communities, taken together, would form the nation's biggest bird sanctuary.

Audubon is also instituting an initiative called Putting Working Lands to Work for Birds and People. This program focuses on forests,

A waterfowl
impoundment
in northeastern
North Carolina

grasslands, farms, and ranches along the Atlantic flyway, the route migrating birds take along the Eastern Seaboard. It will develop management plans for these areas that will provide the best possible habitats for the most vulnerable forest birds. It will, for example, assist with improving habitat for the Golden-winged Warbler, a species in serious decline, in the North Carolina mountains.

The Nature Conservancy states that its mission is to conserve the lands and waters on which all life depends. In the Carolinas, the Nature Conservancy partners with other organizations and agencies to protect lands important to birds. For example, at Fort Bragg, the organization has helped to restore the endangered North Carolina Sandhills population of the Red-cockaded Woodpecker. The Nature Conservancy has also worked with the Marine Corps and conservation partners to protect over 65,000 acres around the Camp Lejeune and Cherry Point military bases.

Over forty land trusts in the Carolinas, from the mountains to the coast, work with landowners to conserve undeveloped lands, thus providing habitat for many species of birds. These land trusts are legal entities entrusted by a property owner with legal ownership or management of the land; the goal of conservation land trusts is to protect wildlife and natural resources. The Congaree Land Trust, for example, has conserved around 72,000 acres (representing 150 properties) in thirteen central South Carolina counties.

Individual Efforts

Residents of the Carolinas have a long history of attracting birds. Early settlers likely baited waterfowl and turkeys to make harvesting the birds easier. With the advent of waterfowl hunting as a sport, wealthy coastal landowners began to convert Low Country rice fields into the earliest waterfowl impoundments. Today, impoundments planted with grain crops are a popular way to attract waterfowl, and crops such as chufa are regularly planted to attract Wild Turkeys. It has also long been a practice in the South Carolina Low Country to plant food plots for bobwhites.

A Wood Duck box with a predator guard

Backyard bird feeding is a very different endeavor. Here food is provided for songbirds simply to bring them closer to our homes so we can enjoy their presence. My (Jim's) mother regularly fed birds in her yard as early as the late 1930s. She had never heard of buying birdseed. She fed her birds scraps, especially leftover bread. It disappeared quickly, and there were always red birds ("cardinals" nowadays) and Blue Jays hanging around. Most folks in small towns had chickens in those days, and they often shared their chicken feed (usually cracked corn) with their backyard birds.

Erecting birdhouses is another activity with very old roots. Before Europeans arrived in the Americas, Native Americans hung gourds for Purple Martins to nest in. Providing shelter for birds even helped save Wood Ducks in the 1930s. Apparently abundant in colonial times, Wood Duck populations had declined to very low numbers by the early 1900s. A strong effort to restore this species, which once nested exclusively in natural cavities in trees, included the first placement of nest boxes in the 1930s. Wood Ducks readily used these nest boxes, and sportsman's clubs, Boy Scout troops, and others began to place thousands of them along creeks and swamps throughout much of the eastern United States. That effort helped reverse the decline of Wood Ducks, and now woodies are one of the most abundant ducks in the Carolinas.

But despite its old roots, the widespread construction of backyard birdhouses didn't begin until the 1970s, when it was part of an effort to combat a serious decline in the number of Eastern Bluebirds, which was at least partly due to a lack of suitable shelter. Since then, there has been

A Jack Finch–built
bluebird house

a tremendous effort to build and place bluebird houses in backyards and
along bluebird trails (a series of bluebird houses spaced 300 feet apart).

Jack Finch of Bailey, North Carolina, began building bluebird houses
in the 1970s and went on to found a nonprofit organization called Homes
for Bluebirds to continue his work. Finch and his organization built and
distributed over 60,000 bluebird houses. Now most Eastern Bluebirds
nest in artificial houses, with only a small percentage of the bluebird
population using old woodpecker holes and other natural cavities.

Frank Newell of Warrenton, North Carolina, also began building bluebird houses because he was concerned about the decline in Eastern Bluebirds. The organization he created, the Eastern Bluebird Rescue Group, has now built and distributed over 265,000 bluebird houses at this writing. They provide these houses at cost.

Bluebird houses are also readily used by other cavity-nesting birds. Chickadees and titmice in particular like the houses, and they may also be used occasionally by Red-bellied Woodpeckers, Northern Flickers, and Great-crested Flycatchers, among others. Two nonnative species, the House Sparrow and European Starling, also compete for these houses.

There is currently a push to provide nest boxes for the Brown-headed Nuthatch, a species of the pine woodlands that is declining because of loss of habitat, particularly the dead trees where they normally excavate their nest cavities.

A Brown-headed Nuthatch at a nest box

Many of us in the Carolinas have decided to make our living spaces, small or large, more attractive to our avian neighbors. With the human population growing rapidly and spreading into formerly wild spaces, the range and quality of birds' natural habitats are changing radically. We urgently need to expand our efforts to make our living spaces better suited for our bird neighbors. This volume will explore this concept and, we hope, provide ideas for making your own part of the Carolinas more bird friendly.

A fog-bound
coniferous
forest in western
North Carolina

Major Ecosystems in the Carolinas

1

The two Carolinas collectively offer a very diverse set of living conditions for birds. In the highest of our mountains, the climate and habitats are very similar to those found in Canada. The Low Country of South Carolina, on the other hand, is subtropical—much like the habitats more commonly associated with Florida. In between these extremes are many subclimates, providing differing habitats for a diverse avifauna.

The highest peaks of the Blue Ridge Mountains in the Carolinas, above 5,000 feet, are primarily forested with stands of red spruce and Fraser fir. Here winters are much colder and summers much cooler than in the rest of the Carolinas. In summer, these forests are home to Winter Wrens, Golden-crowned Kinglets, Veeries, and other birds more commonly associated with forests farther north. These forests are limited in extent, and most are in public ownership. Efforts to attract birds here are generally limited to addressing serious threats to the forests themselves.

Just downslope from the highest forests there is a broad band of mostly deciduous forest that is the summer home for many species, including the Chestnut-sided Warbler, Canada Warbler, Scarlet Tanager, and Ruffed Grouse. While much of the forest is also in public ownership, this portion of the mountains, in addition to having a scattering of towns and some agricultural development, has seen a great increase in the number of summer and retirement homes. Many homeowners here are striving to make their properties more attractive to birds.

The foothills retain some deciduous forest, but here there has been more clearing and second growth, and there are more pines. There's also more farmland here, as well as several large reservoirs. Mountain streams begin to slow and meander in the foothills, and floodplains begin to widen. In recent years some farmland has reverted to forest.

Moving east, the foothills grade into the Piedmont, a densely populated region with several large cities. Much of the original deciduous forest here has been cleared for farmland and pasture, although recently there has been some reforestation. Rivers slow even more and often meander across relatively wide floodplains, much of which is still forested. There are several large reservoirs, which provide habitat for a variety of birds including Ospreys, and waterfowl in winter. Several large tracts of

Spring in the deciduous forests of the Carolina mountains

A Golden-crowned Kinglet in the mountains in North Carolina

land are in public ownership (such as parks and natural areas), and much of this is forested.

The line between the Piedmont and the Coastal Plain represents the westernmost incursion of the Atlantic Ocean. In southeastern North Carolina and northeastern South Carolina there is a region along this transition that's dominated by sandy soils and, traditionally, longleaf pine forests: the Carolina Sandhills. This is one of the important areas for the endangered Red-cockaded Woodpecker. This habitat still has sizable tracts of the longleaf pine forests, although much of the area has been converted to farmland.

East of the Piedmont and Sandhills, the land slopes gradually to the

Old-field broomsedge in the North Carolina Piedmont

A longleaf pine forest in the South Carolina Sandhills

coast. Here the rivers meander even more over wide floodplains, and in the lower reaches of these rivers are large swamps that are home to such species as Prothonotary Warblers, Acadian Flycatchers, and Wood Ducks. While much of the land has been converted to farmland, there are still extensive forests, almost all of which are second growth.

Closer to the coast, salt water begins to intrude up the coastal rivers, and brackish and salt marshes occupy the lower areas. Here such birds as rails and several species of herons and egrets are at home. These marshes give way along the coast to a series of brackish bays and sounds that are home at various times of year for many kinds of birds, including several gull and tern species and many kinds of waterfowl. A series

A salt marsh at Huntington Beach State Park in South Carolina

A flooded swamp in southeastern North Carolina

of barrier islands separates these bodies of water from the open ocean. These islands may be less than a mile from the mainland through most of South Carolina and in North Carolina up to Pamlico Sound. Pamlico Sound separates the mainland from the Outer Banks by as much as twenty-five miles.

These coastal bays and marshes have long been the winter home for waterfowl, and in summer long-legged waders are abundant. Shorebirds stop here to rest and feed during their long migrations between their winter and summer homes. This diverse and abundant birdlife has led people in the region to develop many ways to attract birds. It is here that early settlers on coastal plantations made the first efforts to attract

waterfowl, and now the region features several wildlife refuges, parks, and sanctuaries.

The barrier islands that separate the coastal marshes and bays from the Atlantic Ocean have undergone tremendous development over the last century, but the maritime forests and beaches are still important to migrating birds, and the beaches are the traditional nesting grounds for several species of shorebirds and terns, including Willets, American Oystercatchers, and Least Terns. Several refuges and parks have been established to protect key portions of the beaches.

The nearshore Atlantic Ocean is also important for many species of birds. Brown Pelicans, gulls, terns, and some waterfowl feed in the nearshore waters, and pelagic species such as Northern Gannets and shearwaters are regular visitors offshore. These areas need to be protected to ensure that this significant portion of birdlife continues to find conditions favorable for occupation.

The complexity of climate in the Carolinas and the resulting range of habitats result in a very diverse avifauna. Over 470 species of birds have been recorded in the Carolinas, and many of these nest in some part of the two states. This offers those of us who live here the opportunity to see and attract many species to our properties. Which species we can entice depends on, first, the kinds of efforts we make to fulfill their requirements for living space. It also depends on the habitats on our properties and nearby. While birds are highly mobile, if a small area of appropriate habitat is widely separated from larger areas, they may not find or utilize it.

Cape Point on the Outer Banks in North Carolina

Birds' Basic Needs

2

Birds share the same needs as most animals, including us. They need clean, safe places to live, adequate food and water, shelter from environmental extremes, and a safe place to raise their young.

Habitat

When we talk about a place for birds to live, we often use the term "habitat." Habitat is an ecological concept that describes places for animals to live in terms of the plant community they occupy. Thus, the spruce-fir forests of our high mountains and the cypress swamps of our lowlands are both considered habitats. They are usually described in terms of the kinds of plants they contain. If the physical parameters, such as soil type and availability of water, are also considered, we use the term "ecosystem."

Birds tend to occupy those habitats where they find all of the things that they require to survive and reproduce. For example, we would expect to find woodpeckers in forest habitats and not in salt marsh habitats. We find Wood Ducks along streams and in coastal swamps but not in high-mountain spruce-fir forests.

Any given habitat is typically home to many different species of birds. Within a habitat there are different kinds of food, different opportunities for nest placement, and a range of other things birds need to survive and reproduce. Each species occupying this habitat tends to utilize the portion of the habitat where it is most efficient. For example, one species may be most efficient at feeding on insects in the canopy of the forest, while another species is most efficient at finding seeds on the forest floor. This minimizes competition for resources and allows many species to occupy the same habitat. The subunits of habitat are referred to as "niches." Thus, in the deciduous mountain forests, the Blackburnian Warbler, an insect eater in the canopy, and the Ovenbird, an insect eater near and on the ground, occupy different niches.

To survive and remain healthy, each bird—or, during the nesting season, each pair of birds—must have an adequate amount of appropriate habitat. Exactly what amount this is varies considerably among species. For small birds, such as warblers, a few acres of appropriate habitat may meet all their needs, while a Red-tailed Hawk or a Wild Turkey will require a much larger area.

A male Blackburnian Warbler in the mountains of North Carolina

The most critical times of the year for Carolina birds are the nesting season (spring and summer) and winter. In the nesting season, an adult or pair of adults must be able to obtain adequate food for themselves and for their families. In winter, birds spend more energy keeping warm and therefore require more food. At these times the quality of the habitat becomes especially critical.

Migrating birds must pay particular attention to habitat because they have to find adequate food and cover during the sometimes very long trips between their summer and winter homes.

Territory

During the nesting season, most small male birds establish territories that they defend against other male birds of the same species. This ensures that only one set of offspring of each species will be reared in each unit of habitat.

You can rather easily see this in the birds nesting in your yards or in nearby habitats. On a warm spring day, get out a lawn chair, a cool drink, and a pad of paper and sketch out your surroundings, showing the houses, trees, and major shrub beds. Then note where the singing birds are located. If you have cardinals in your neighborhood, they are a good choice for this exercise because they are persistent singers with relatively loud voices. You will soon see that each male has several sing-

A colony of nesting Royal Terns

ing locations; taken together, these locations show the bird's territory. Other males may sing from nearby locations, but each is moving around the perimeter of its chosen territory, warning other singing males to keep out.

Within each territory the male courts a female, and together they build a nest and rear their young, without interference or competition from other males. Usually males defend their territory only against other reproductively active males of the same species, so males of other species—if you're tracking cardinals, perhaps Blue Jays or Carolina Chickadees—may have overlapping territories. Sometimes birds make exceptions around feeders: several males may flock to a feeder inside one male's territory.

This kind of territoriality is the most common type among birds, but some birds do it differently. Some species, like gulls, terns, herons, egrets, and ibis, defend only the nest itself and thus have very small territories. While most birds in the Carolinas are monogamous (one male and one female form a pair and raise a family), some are polygynous (a single male pairs with more than one female). In such cases each female builds a nest within the territory and rears the young, so the adult males actively defend territories that may include more than one nest. Red-winged Blackbirds are an example of a species that is often polygynous.

Cover

A basic feature of habitat is cover. While birds are adapted to living in the open, they need shelter when weather conditions become extreme, as in winter, and they need escape cover in order to elude predators. In summer, cover is seldom an issue in the Carolinas; there is usually plenty of plant growth to provide shelter from all but the most extreme weather, cover for nests, and escape cover when predators appear. Some habitats are primarily vegetated by deciduous plants, however, and in winter these plants provide much less cover than in summer. Habitats with at least some evergreen vegetation generally provide better cover in winter.

Food

Birds typically have high metabolic rates and need food high in energy. Most birds eat either animal matter, such as insects and worms, or energy-rich plant matter such as fruits and seeds.

While the avian digestive system is generally efficient, in some species that feed primarily on plant material, the young chicks must eat easier-to-digest animal matter until their digestive systems are more developed. For example, adult cardinals primarily eat seeds and fruit, but they feed their nestlings mostly insects. Such young also need the additional protein found in animal matter to support their rapid growth and feather development. The Gray Catbird on the facing page, which had its nest in a blackberry tangle, was observed bringing insects to its chicks

A Gray Catbird feeding nestlings

A Prothonotary Warbler bathing

and then stopping to eat a berry or two on its way from the nest to find more animal food for the chicks.

As their digestive systems develop, the chicks shift to the same foods adults eat, and so you may see adult cardinals at your feeder passing sunflower seeds to youngsters developed enough to digest them but still young enough to beg their parents to feed them.

ABOVE
A Northern
Cardinal taking
a shower under
a mister

RIGHT
A female American
Redstart at a
birdbath with a
drip fountain

Water

Birds need an adequate supply of clean water for drinking, and many birds also like to bathe regularly, especially during hot weather. You can provide water for birds in many ways. Most basic is the traditional birdbath, usually a shallow container placed in the open but with escape cover nearby. Do not place your birdbath so close to cover that the neighbor's cat can use it as ambush cover, but do have it close enough that your bathers can dive into cover should a hawk appear. Birdbaths should be about two inches deep, with flat rocks placed near the edge to provide shallower places for smaller birds.

If you have an outdoor faucet close to your bath, consider adding a drip fountain, which seems to attract birds to the bath; chickadees love to drink directly from the drip. Many birds also love to take shower baths. Try adding a mister to your setup and activate it on hot summer days so that it sends a fine mist over an open shrub or tree limb. You'll be able to watch the birds gather like kids at the swimming pool on a hot summer day.

Backyard water gardens may also be utilized by birds. Make sure that there are shallow places where birds can drink and bathe. Ponds can

also attract animal food for birds, such as frogs, tadpoles, and insects, and can be stocked with small species of fish.

If you have space enough for a pond or impoundment, you may be able to attract a variety of waterbirds. Ponds are generally permanent and range in size from less than an acre to many acres. If a pond is stocked with fish, wading birds such as herons and egrets will often visit, especially if the pond has shallow edges not overgrown with vegetation. Wood Duck boxes installed on posts over water may attract nesting woodies, especially if the pond is near a creek or swamp.

Unlike ponds, impoundments are generally temporary: the site is drained in late winter and planted to crops attractive to waterfowl. These impoundments are most commonly built to attract waterfowl to be hunted, and federal laws allow hunting over planted crops so long as the crops remain standing. But impoundments work just as well for folks who only want to attract waterfowl to their property because they enjoy seeing them.

The Annual
Cycle of Birds

3

Carolina birds are divided into several groups based on travel and residence patterns. Some birds are permanent residents, living in the same general region throughout the year. Others are resident only in the summer and migrate further south for the winter, and some do the reverse, spending summers farther north and moving to the Carolinas for the winter. Still another group spends summers farther north and winters farther south, only passing through the Carolinas in spring and fall. Thus, the annual life cycles of our birds vary somewhat depending on their residence status.

The annual cycle of the Carolinas' permanent-resident and summer-resident birds can be effectively divided into breeding and nonbreeding periods. Breeding must take place when environmental conditions are the most conducive to the production of eggs and the rearing of offspring. For most bird species in the Carolinas, that's from April through August. The nonbreeding period encompasses the remainder of the year; birds that are only summer residents of the Carolinas spend this period elsewhere. During the breeding period, birds devote much of their efforts and energy to the production of offspring.

Most scientists believe that the increase in the amount of daylight in late winter and early spring stimulates the production of hormones in birds, which causes the gonads to enlarge in preparation for breeding. As males achieve reproductive condition, they search out and establish a suitable territory that provides cover for nest sites as well as access to adequate food. The males then begin to sing around the periphery of their territory to proclaim their dominance of the area, from which other males of the same species are now excluded. In more open habitats, males often perform both elaborate displays and vocalizations to establish territory. When a female bird encounters a suitable male with a quality territory, the pairing process begins.

In some bird species that are winter residents in the Carolinas, the pair bonds between males and females begin to form long before they migrate to the breeding grounds. Winter-resident birds that will be moving north for the summer may begin courtship prior to departing the Carolinas. You will see these birds molting into their breeding plumage, and you may hear the males beginning to practice their courtship songs.

A male Swainson's Warbler singing in his territory

A male Northern
Cardinal in
the snow

In most cases pair bonds will not be fully formed until the birds reach
their summer quarters, but in waterfowl, courtship and pair bonding
usually takes place on the winter grounds, and the birds depart for more
northern nesting areas as mated pairs.

Once the pairing process is complete, males and females copulate.

The Annual Cycle of Birds

Then the female constructs a nest, with the male assisting in many species. When egg-laying is complete, the female typically incubates the clutch of eggs until they hatch, again with the help of the male in some species. Sometimes the male feeds the female while she sits on the eggs, and in other cases he incubates the eggs as she seeks her own food.

When the eggs hatch, usually in April, May, and June, the voracious nestlings begin to solicit food from the adults, and both parents must work diligently throughout the day to provide sufficient food for the rapidly growing young. Large quantities of protein (usually insects) are necessary to fuel the production and molting of feathers in nestlings, as well as the increase in body mass. During this time adult males may stop singing so that predators are not attracted to the nests and young.

After the breeding period ends, most species begin to molt, and migratory species begin the sometimes very long flights to the winter quarters. For instance, the American Golden Plover in the fall migrates from the tundra in northern Canada and Alaska to South America, where it overwinters on the Pampas in Argentina. In the spring, this species migrates north through central North America until it reaches the breeding grounds in the Arctic. This round trip approaches 5,000 miles. As part of the post-breeding activity to prepare for migration, birds feed constantly in a process known as "pre-migratory hyperphagia." During migration most birds must continue to feed heavily to provide the energy needed for the long flights and thus must find appropriate habitat with good food supplies along the way.

For birds that winter in the Carolinas, competition for declining food increases dramatically even as they need more energy for thermoregulation during very cold periods, and social dominance becomes extremely important in acquiring food. The cooperative behavior between males and females that characterized the breeding period changes when food resources are limited and temperatures are low. Studies on sex- and age-related dominance in nonbreeding songbirds have shown that female and young birds are often forced to feed in inferior habitats where higher mortality may occur. Often only the males and fittest females survive the nonbreeding season and again begin courtship and nesting as a new nesting season begins.

Feeding Birds

4

The most basic habitat features to consider when attempting to attract birds to your yard (or anywhere else) are food, water, and shelter. Chapter 2 talked about providing water and shelter, but often our first effort is to provide food by way of a bird feeder, and this chapter will explore this in more detail.

The Avian Digestive System

Before we look at the different kinds of bird feeders and food, it helps to understand how birds digest their food.

Birds lack teeth and so do not chew their food. Food is broken or torn by the beak and then swallowed into an enlarged area of the esophagus called the crop. The crop is primarily a storage organ that holds undigested food, allowing birds to feed quickly and then escape to a more sheltered place, limiting their exposure to predators. Further down the esophagus, most birds have a muscular organ called a gizzard. Here hard food items, such as seeds, are ground into smaller particles. Food passes from the gizzard to the stomach, where digestion continues, and then to the intestines, where most absorption of food into the bloodstream occurs. Waste material passes to the cloaca, a storage organ where residues from the digestive system and the urinary system collect before they are eliminated.

The avian digestive system is generally rapid and efficient. In birds that eat primarily insects, such as warblers, food may be processed and undigested waste voided in as little as twenty minutes. Birds that eat seeds, which must be ground up by a gizzard, require more time to process a meal. Gizzards in some species, such as Wild Turkeys, are remarkable organs, able to grind up whole acorns and even hickory nuts. These birds also improve the gizzard's function by ingesting gravel, which helps grind hard food items in the gizzard.

What Do Birds Eat?

As a general rule, birds eat foods that are high in calories. Flying requires tremendous amounts of energy, and birds' metabolisms are generally very high. Many birds therefore eat protein-rich animal matter such as insects or fish for growth and maintenance. Plant eaters usually

A Red-eyed
Vireo eating a
beautyberry

A female
Prothonotary
Warbler with
a caterpillar

consume calorie-dense seeds, berries, and fruits rather than leaves or stems, though some species, including many waterfowl, do feed on leaves and stems. It is interesting that many birds, such as Northern Cardinals, eat primarily a variety of fruits and seeds but feed their nestlings insects and other invertebrates. Apparently the digestive systems of these youngsters cannot yet digest seeds but can handle the easier-to-digest animal matter. As the young grow, they shift to a diet similar to that of the adults.

Hummingbirds regularly feed on nectar, which is high in calories but lacks nutrients. Thus hummers also regularly eat small insects to obtain protein, minerals, and other essential nutrients.

Preferred Feeder Foods

Evening Grosbeaks
at a feeder

STRIPED SUNFLOWER SEEDS

Northern Cardinal

BLACK OIL SUNFLOWER SEEDS

Brown-headed Nuthatch
Carolina Chickadee
Evening Grosbeak
Northern Cardinal
Tufted Titmouse

PEANUTS

Blue Jay

CRACKED CORN

Eastern Towhee
Mourning Dove
White-throated Sparrow

NYJER

American Goldfinch

WHITE PROSO MILLET

Mourning Dove
Painted Bunting
White-throated Sparrow

MEALWORMS

Eastern Bluebird

SUET MIXES

Blue Jay
Brown Thrasher
Carolina Chickadee
Carolina Wren
Nuthatches
Pine Warbler
Ruby-crowned Kinglet
Tufted Titmouse
Woodpeckers
Yellow-rumped Warbler
Yellow-throated Warbler

An American holly
with ripe berries

Plants or Feeders?

There are two basic ways we can provide food for birds: we can grow plants that will provide food, or we can offer supplemental food in bird feeders. Let's look at both options.

Using berry- and seed-producing plants in landscape designs or as food plots is a great way to attract many species of birds. Hollies and other berry-producing plants can fit into most landscape plans and provide natural beauty as well as cover and food for birds. When space is available, as on farms, it is a great idea to plant food plots both for songbirds and for game species such as Wild Turkeys, Mourning Doves, and bobwhites. Where shallow impoundments can be created, food plots may also attract waterfowl.

There is a strong push today to use native plants that are adapted to local conditions rather than nonnative plants in suburban landscapes. In fact, even if you stock bird feeders, it is a good practice to rely heavily on native plants in your landscapes. The insects hosted by native plants are generally more diverse and more abundant than those hosted by nonnative species, and this provides more food for your avian neighbors. Planting annuals such as cosmos, zinnias, and sunflowers can do double or even triple duty for birds: the flowers provide nectar for hummingbirds while the seeds provide food for seed eaters such as American Goldfinches and a variety of sparrows. In addition, the flowers attract and provide nectar for a variety of butterflies. If you leave the plants during the winter, seed-eating birds will continue to forage beneath the spent plants.

Another way plants provide food for birds is by attracting insects

OPPOSITE
A Northern
Cardinal eating
a beautyberry

A cardinal
flower plant

Suggested Food Plants

TREES

American basswood (*Tilia americana*)
American beech (*Fagus grandifolia*)
American holly (*Ilex opaca*)
Black cherry (*Prunus serotina*)
    (also good for insect larvae)
Black gum (*Nyssa sylvatica*)
Chickasaw plums (*Prunus angustifolia*)
Flowering dogwood (*Cornus florida*)
Native oaks (*Quercus* spp.)
    (also good for insect larvae)
Persimmon (*Diospyros virginiana*)
River birch (*Betula nigra*)
Sassafras (*Sassafras albidum*)
Serviceberry (*Amelanchier laevis*)

SHRUBS

American beautyberry (*Callicarpa americana*)
Blueberries (*Vaccinium* spp.)
Red elderberry (*Sambucus racemosa*)
Staghorn sumac (*Rhus typhina*)

PERENNIALS

Blackberries (*Rubus* spp.)
Butterfly weed (*Asclepias tuberosa*)
Fire pinks (*Silene virginica*)
Joe-pye weed (*Eutrochium fistulosum*)
Purple coneflower (*Echinacea purpurea*)

ANNUALS

Black-eyed Susans (*Rudbeckia hirta*)
Garden cosmos (*Cosmos bipinnatus*)
Sunflowers (*Helianthus* spp.)
Tickseed (*Coreopsis* spp.)

GOOD NECTAR PRODUCERS

Bee balm (*Monarda* spp.)
Blazing star (*Liatris spicata*)
Cardinal flower (*Lobelia cardinalis*)
Coral honeysuckle (*Lonicera sempervirens*)
Salvia (*Salvia* spp.)
Trumpet vine (*Campsis radicans*)

PLANTS SUITABLE FOR FOOD PLOTS

Chufa (*Cyperus esculentus*)
Clover (*Trifolium* spp.)
Corn (*Zea mays*)
Japanese millet (*Echinochloa esculenta*)
Millet (*Pennisetum* spp.)
Milo (*Sorghum bicolor*)
Soybeans (*Glycine max*)
Sunflowers, especially black oil varieties (*Helianthus* spp.)

Sunflowers

For more detailed recommendations, visit these websites:

www.audubon.org/native-plants
https://content.ces.ncsu.edu/managing-backyards-and-other
    -urban-habitats-for-birds

Zinnias

(especially caterpillars), which then become food for insect-eating birds. If you grow native plants, you will most likely get good populations of caterpillars. This is perhaps a difficult idea for those who are gardeners and have an inherent dislike for foliage-eating caterpillars. But your birds will enjoy them, and it's likely that you won't notice much damage to the plants. Birds such as chickadees eat huge numbers of caterpillars and feed lots of them to their chicks, so they eat most of the caterpillars before they get large enough to do significant damage.

But feeding birds by planting certain plants isn't the most common approach. When we think of feeding birds, we usually think of providing feeders stocked with foods relished by particular species. We suspect that the basic feeder in most yards is stocked with either a birdseed mix or sunflower seeds. This is certainly not a bad way to start. The standard birdseed mix usually contains white millet, milo, cracked corn, wheat, and black oil sunflower seeds, which will attract a variety of seed-eating birds. But often such mixes are heavy on the less expensive (and often less palatable) seeds and short on the more nutritious seeds.

It is probably a better idea to provide at least two and perhaps three or four feeders, each stocked with a single kind of seed. Start with a feeder stocked with black oil sunflower seeds, or, if you have lots of cardinals, you might mix black oil and striped sunflower seeds in a single feeder. This will be attractive to most of your resident seed eaters, such as cardinals, chickadees, and titmice. If you live in goldfinch country,

add a feeder stocked with thistle. In coastal areas, from about Morehead City, North Carolina, south, by all means add a tube feeder stocked with white proso millet for Painted Buntings.

A female Painted Bunting at a tube feeder

Types of Feeders

There are many kinds of feeders that hold and dispense seeds while at the same time protecting the seeds from the weather. The kind you choose will depend on your preference, the kinds of seeds being offered, the species that you wish to feed, and the species that you do not wish to feed.

An open-shelf feeder works just fine for holding a limited amount of feed, and one with a roof will offer protection from the weather. It will not, however, limit access by larger birds, such as grackles, or feeder raiders, like gray and red squirrels. Tube feeders surrounded by wire cages are a good bet to store and provide seeds, protect them from the weather, and limit access for larger birds and perhaps squirrels. We have to say "perhaps" for squirrels because they are masters at defeating feeders designed to keep them out.

Some birds do not like to feed at elevated feeders. Species like White-throated Sparrows, Eastern Towhees, Dark-eyed Juncos, and Mourning Doves will come readily to cracked corn or millet placed on the ground but will seldom visit elevated feeders. Scatter seeds on the ground under

Suet Recipes

There are a variety of suet mixes available commercially, but we like to make our own with a recipe we've modified from one we found in *Organic Gardening* magazine in the mid-1990s. The birds love it. We usually ration them to one cake (¼ to ½ pound) daily. We often use natural suet feeders, such as a section of a dead branch, as shown opposite, but a wire suet holder will work fine.

Makes about 1 dozen (3-inch-diameter) cakes

3 cups cornmeal
1 cup cracked corn or birdseed (we use a general seed mix)
1 cup oatmeal
1 cup peanut butter
1 cup shortening
1 cup whole wheat flour

Mix all the ingredients together in a large bowl by hand or with a stand mixer or handheld mixer. Shape the mixture into cakes that will work with your suet feeder. Place the cakes in airtight containers and chill in the refrigerator overnight to firm before placing them in your feeder. Store in the refrigerator for up to six months.

A recipe by Lena Gallitano is also well liked by her birds. These suet cakes will fit into standard wire suet holders.

4 cups cornmeal
4 cups quick-cooking rolled oats
2 cups flour
2 cups crunchy peanut butter
2 cups lard
⅔ cup sugar

Place all the ingredients in a large saucepan over medium heat and stir until well blended. Pour the mixture into a 9 x 13-inch pan and spread it out evenly. Cover and refrigerate overnight. Cut the suet into squares to fit your suet feeder and store in an airtight container in the refrigerator or freezer for up to six months.

Note: If your suet feeder does not exclude squirrels, you may wish to use a commercial product that includes hot peppers, or add a heavy sprinkling of cayenne pepper to either of the above mixes. The birds do not seem to mind, and the squirrels seem to avoid it.

A Red-bellied Woodpecker at a natural suet feeder

A red squirrel on
a tube feeder

your elevated feeders to attract these species. Of course, in this case you will have to share with the squirrels.

Suet mixes attract a variety of birds but are especially attractive to species that are primarily insect eaters. Woodpeckers, nuthatches, and wrens will visit regularly, and Carolina Chickadees and Tufted Titmice also love such feeders. Pine, Yellow-throated, and Yellow-rumped Warblers also visit our suet feeders in winter when other food is scarce. Even species such as cardinals, which we think of as seed eaters, will visit suet feeders. This may be because suet mixes often contain whole seeds, and peanut butter is a regular ingredient. Suet mixes can be purchased individually, or you can mix a batch at home, store it in the fridge, and dole it out as needed. We put ours up in quarter-pound cakes and have to ration our birds to one cake a day.

There are several more exotic foods and feeders designed to attract specific species. Historically, folks in the coastal zone of the Carolinas have been putting out grape jelly, pound cake, and orange halves in a

variety of ways to attract Baltimore Orioles. A few of these orioles are winter residents in the Coastal Plain, and if you are lucky, these foods may attract and hold your orioles for the winter. Be sure to get your offerings out by early October, when the orioles arrive in the region.

Always place your feeder in an area where you can enjoy the birds while they dine. Clean your feeders frequently with warm water and let them dry completely before refilling. You may also wish to occasionally clean them with a mild bleach solution. This will help to avoid a buildup of pathogens that could make your birds sick.

Feeder Raiders

A major problem with bird feeders is that they're raided by mammals such as raccoons and especially squirrels. If you enjoy watching the raccoons and squirrels, do nothing, but if you would prefer not to have them eat food you've put out for the birds and damage or destroy your

A male White-throated Sparrow feeding beneath an elevated feeder

A hanging sunflower feeder with a squirrel excluder

A Red-bellied Woodpecker at a natural suet feeder

feeders, there are some things you can do. Several types of feeders are designed to prevent large birds or mammals such as squirrels from getting to the food. Some may even work. If you have one that does, you are fortunate, or perhaps your squirrels are not as crafty as some. In most cases, anything less than an all-out effort to prevent these agile critters will fail.

A solid solution is to place a large cone-shaped baffle called a predator guard above a feeder that hangs from a limb or below a feeder placed on a post. The cone should be at least two and preferably three feet in diameter and made of galvanized metal or aluminum (for details on constructing a predator guard, see the sidebar in chapter 6). The small ones often seen in bird supply stores usually will not suffice, and even the large ones will not deter black bears, which occasionally raid feeders in more remote locations.

OPPOSITE
A male Baltimore Oriole

Case Studies: How Birds Are Attracted and Protected throughout the Carolinas

5

People, organizations, and agencies work to attract birds in a wide variety of settings across the Carolinas. These efforts range from state-wide projects to rebuild populations of a species, to wildlife refuges encompassing thousands of acres, to the placement of a feeder on the balcony of a downtown apartment. In this chapter we will look at some examples of the many ways we attract birds.

Species-Specific Projects

There are several regional efforts across the Carolinas to restore populations of species currently or recently in decline. Wild Turkeys, Golden-winged Warblers, and Red-cockaded Woodpeckers have all required these kinds of endeavors to return them to earlier numbers or to maintain declining populations.

Wild Turkey Restoration

Wild Turkeys were once widespread in the Carolinas, but by the early 1900s their numbers had dropped dramatically, and the birds were found only in small numbers in localized areas. Projects to return these birds to their earlier numbers were begun in both Carolinas in the 1950s. Some early efforts that involved releasing pen-raised birds failed, but conservationists found success in moving wild birds from areas where they were still present in good numbers to areas without birds.

At present, due primarily to the work of the South Carolina Department of Natural Resources and the North Carolina Wildlife Resources Commission, with help from other agencies and organizations, there are good numbers of Wild Turkeys throughout both states. This is a classic example of how a species in danger of being extirpated from a region can come back from the brink if public opinion is on their side and public agencies, private organizations, and individual landowners combine their efforts.

Snow Geese feeding in cornfield stubble

47

Feeding birds and providing birdhouses are common ways of attracting birds in the Carolinas.

American Goldfinches and Red Crossbills at a sunflower seed feeder

A male Tree Swallow at a nest box

Wild Turkeys foraging in a food plot

A feeding Wild Turkey flock with a strutting tom

Golden-Winged Warbler Habitat Management

Golden-winged Warbler numbers are declining drastically in the southern Appalachians, but the second-growth forests at midlevels in the mountains of western North Carolina are one of their remaining strongholds. These warblers build their nests in young, brushy forests and shrubland, and such areas are limited.

The U.S. Department of Agriculture's Natural Resources Conservation Service, the National Park Service, the National Audubon Society, and the Southern Appalachian Highlands Conservancy, along with other land trusts and private landowners, are working together to increase the amount of nesting habitat for this warbler by creating new forests and maintaining forests in their early stages, beyond the usual time frame in reforestation. This may involve selectively cutting down trees to encourage the development of shrubby habitats or maintain existing shrub-

A male Golden-winged Warbler

A Golden-winged Warbler nesting habitat in western North Carolina

land. Such selective cutting also benefits other species, such as Indigo Buntings, Eastern Towhees, Prairie Warblers, Chestnut-sided Warblers, and American Woodcock, that also need this kind of plant community. This is a great example of how a concerted effort by public agencies, private organizations, and individuals is making a difference for a species in need of help.

Refuges and Sanctuaries

There are many wildlife refuges and sanctuaries in the Carolinas that are designed to attract and protect birds. Most well-known are the national wildlife refuges, state refuges, wildlife management areas, and game lands, but there are also sanctuaries operated by private agencies. Let's look at some examples.

Mattamuskeet National Wildlife Refuge

The Mattamuskeet National Wildlife Refuge was created in 1934 in Hyde County, North Carolina. It is primarily an old Carolina bay lake that was drained in the early 1900s in a failed effort to turn it into farmland. The federal government purchased the land and turned it into the second national wildlife refuge in North Carolina.

Lake Mattamuskeet is a large but shallow lake; it covers about 50,000 acres but is only a foot or two deep over much of its area. No large streams feed the lake, and water flow in the exit canals that connect the lake to nearby Pamlico Sound is regulated by one-way gates. These gates allow excess water to drain from the lake but do not allow the brackish water from Pamlico Sound to enter the lake.

The lake's shallow, mostly fresh water provides good growing conditions for aquatic plants and allows waterfowl easy access to these plants. The refuge management has also created several shallow impoundments around the perimeter of the lake. Here water levels can be controlled, allowing the impoundments to dry out in summer so that marsh plants that waterfowl feed on can grow. These impoundments can then be flooded in autumn to make the plants accessible to wintering waterfowl.

The lake was once an important wintering area for ducks and geese, and Mattamuskeet became the Canada Goose capital of the world in the 1950s, when more than 100,000 Canada Geese regularly wintered on the refuge. The large flocks of migrant Canada Geese no longer come to Mattamuskeet for the winter; most now stop short at more northern

Wintering Tundra Swans on Lake Mattamuskeet, with the old pumping station in the background

Northern Pintails flush from an impoundment

locations, where changing farming practices have increased their food supply. In recent years, however, they have been replaced by wintering Tundra Swans that have been displaced from Chesapeake Bay. Now Mattamuskeet hosts over 30,000 swans most winters. The swans usually arrive in November and utilize the refuge and the surrounding grain fields until March.

Ducks still come to Mattamuskeet in large numbers, and one may see thousands of Northern Pintails and a variety of other ducks between November and March. A large wintering flock of Snow Geese also roosts on the refuge, often heading out into the surrounding grain fields to feed.

A longleaf pine forest in the Carolina Sandhills National Wildlife Refuge

A controlled burn in a longleaf pine forest in the Carolina Sandhills National Wildlife Refuge

Carolina Sandhills National Wildlife Refuge

The Carolina Sandhills National Wildlife Refuge encompasses some 45,348 acres in Chesterfield County, South Carolina. The refuge headquarters is located 3.1 miles north of McBee on Highway 1. The management for Red-cockaded Woodpeckers on this refuge is an excellent example of how landowners with large tracts can manage their property for both timber harvest and wildlife.

The rolling sandhills provide a diversity of habitats that support some 190 bird species, 42 species of mammals, 41 species of reptiles, and 25 amphibian species. In addition, more than 800 plant species have been recorded there. Two of the most notable animal species are the

Red-cockaded Woodpecker, which is on the federal list of endangered species, and the Pine Barrens tree frog, which the North Carolina Natural Heritage Program considers "significantly rare." This refuge has the largest population of Red-cockaded Woodpeckers in the national wildlife refuge system.

The refuge is composed of some 42,000 acres of woodlands, 30 ponds or lakes, and about 1,400 acres of fields. The sandy soil supports an extensive longleaf pine forest, which is currently managed to restore the historical longleaf pine–wiregrass ecosystem. The basic management strategy involves controlled burns of about 12,000 to 15,000 acres per year and selective timber harvest to improve habitat diversity, especially for the Red-cockaded Woodpecker.

Battery Island

Both Carolinas have extensive coastal sanctuaries designed to attract and protect nesting waterbirds such as pelicans, gulls, terns, herons, and egrets. These sanctuaries are managed by several private, state, and federal agencies. All are important in that they provide safe places for these birds to nest and raise their young.

Battery Island, at the mouth of the Cape Fear River in southeastern

A flock of
White Ibis at
Battery Island

Battery Island,
North Carolina,
seen from the air

North Carolina, is one such sanctuary. The island is owned by the State
of North Carolina, but Audubon North Carolina leases and manages it,
and it is also supported by the Cape Fear Garden Club. Most years the
island hosts the largest group of nesting waterbirds in North Carolina.
Sometimes more than 10,000 pairs of White Ibis and smaller numbers of several heron and egret species nest at Battery Island. American
Oystercatchers and Eastern Willets also nest on the beaches and grassy
swales.

OPPOSITE
Great Egret chicks
in a nest on
Battery Island

Bear Island and Donnelley Wildlife Management Areas

Bear Island and Donnelley Wildlife Management Areas are part of the ACE (Ashepoo-Combahee-Edisto) Basin and are managed by the South Carolina Department of Natural Resources. Bear Island WMA is managed primarily to provide quality habitat for wintering waterfowl with a series of impoundments. It also, however, provides important habitat for migrating shorebirds such as the American Avocet and for herons, egrets, and ibis. Bald Eagles and Ospreys also nest on the site.

Donnelley WMA contains a mixture of wetland and upland habitats and is managed for birds and other wildlife. The water levels in old rice fields are seasonally regulated for waterfowl. In the uplands, there are food plots for birds and other wildlife, and controlled burns make habitats more welcoming for bobwhites, Wild Turkeys, deer, and others.

Both sites have a series of roads that allow access for most of the year. Bear Island has a managed waterfowl-hunting season, and this restricts travel at times. Both sites offer excellent opportunities to view a variety of birds in their natural Low Country habitats.

Francis Beidler Forest

The Francis Beidler Forest in Four Holes Swamp, a blackwater creek system, is a wildlife sanctuary owned and managed by the National Audubon Society. Located off Interstate 26 at exit 187, near Harleyville, South Carolina, about an hour inland from Charleston, it's a magnificent example of how important habitat preservation is for birdlife, with some 148 species recorded. There's an environmental education center at the entrance to a 1.75-mile boardwalk through the sanctuary.

The sanctuary encompasses over 16,000 acres of primarily bald

LEFT
The boardwalk through the cypress-tupelo swamp of the Francis Beidler Forest

ABOVE
A recently burned pine forest in the Donnelley Wildlife Management Area in South Carolina

OPPOSITE
A Greater Yellowlegs in a Bear Island impoundment

A female
Prothonotary
Warbler

cypress and tupelo. About 1,800 acres of this area is old-growth forest. Beidler is purported to be the world's largest virgin cypress-tupelo swamp forest. Some of the cypress trees here seem to reach to the clouds and are said to be over 1,000 years old. The Beidler Forest was designated a national landmark in 1979 and as a Ramsar Wetland of International Importance in 2008.

The Beidler Forest is a pristine sanctuary that's been literally untouched for hundreds of years. Walking along the boardwalk in the spring is a marvelous experience as you see the golden flash of a female Prothonotary Warbler flitting among the cypresses, searching for a suitable nest site. Equally exciting is the foraging behavior of a Yellow-crowned Night Heron as it extracts crayfish from the shallows beneath the massive trees. If you are a careful observer, you may even encounter at close range a Barred Owl watching your every move.

Beaver Lake Bird Sanctuary

The Beaver Lake Bird Sanctuary is located in the suburbs north of Asheville, North Carolina. Established in the mid-1980s, the sanctuary is managed by the Elisha Mitchell Audubon Society, a local chapter of the National Audubon Society. A 0.38-mile boardwalk meanders through several habitats adjacent to the lake, and an overlook provides views of the lake itself. There are interpretive signs along the walk, and the Elisha Mitchell Audubon Society gives regularly scheduled guided walks to view the wildlife. The sanctuary is open to the public, and there is no fee.

The entrance to the Beaver Lake Bird Sanctuary

An interpretive sign at the entrance to the Beaver Lake Bird Sanctuary boardwalk

The lake attracts a variety of waterbirds, and the surrounding wetland forest and marsh attract both resident and migrant birds.

The Beaver Lake Bird Sanctuary is a great example of how local groups can protect important habitats and educate the public about birds.

Parks and Gardens

Parks of all sizes stretch across the Carolinas, and most attract birds—sometimes simply by providing a variety of habitats, and sometimes by actively feeding birds and providing nest boxes.

View of Beaver
Lake from the
boardwalk

Lake Conestee
wetlands

Lake Conestee Nature Preserve

The Lake Conestee Nature Preserve is located in Greenville County, South Carolina, and encompasses some 400 acres. This preserve had its genesis in the early 1890s, when a rock dam was constructed on the Reedy River, creating a 130-acre lake to facilitate industrial activities. The lake was very important in the early industrial growth of Greenville, but industrial waste and sediments from the various industries and the city of Greenville began to contaminate and fill the lake. It is now nearly filled with sediments and is characterized primarily as bottomland forest and wetlands.

Today the preserve is owned by the Conestee Foundation and managed by the Greenville County Recreation District. A diversity of habitat types makes up the preserve, including pine and mixed deciduous forest, a transitional meadow, the Reedy River, and extensive wetlands. Six miles of paved trails and six miles of natural trails give visitors access to these habitats. In addition, the park has more than 4,000 feet of boardwalks and decks. The National Audubon Society has recognized this diverse ecological community as a Global Important Bird Area, and the Greenville County Bird Club has recorded over 200 bird species, including a variety of waterfowl, wading birds, and songbirds. The Rusty Blackbird, a species that winters in swampy places, has overwintered here for many years. The species has undergone a precipitous decline in numbers over the last four decades, which makes the park important for these blackbirds. This beautiful natural area is also home to a variety of mammals, including beavers, otters, and raccoons. A variety of turtles, snakes, lizards, and frogs also make their homes in both the wetland and upland habitats.

Swan Lake Iris Gardens

Swan Lake Iris Gardens is an excellent example of how a seminatural habitat within city limits can be transformed into an extremely attractive area for birds. This park had its genesis in 1927 when businessman Hamilton Carr Bland bought some swampland next to West Liberty Street in Sumter, South Carolina. Mr. Bland began building a fishpond

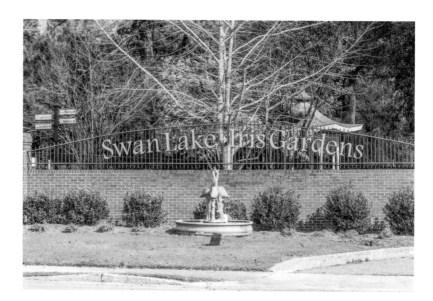

The entrance
to Swan Lake
Iris Gardens

and bird sanctuary, and during the pond's construction, he deposited some Japanese iris bulbs along the banks of the pond. All these years later, irises still bloom there in abundance each year in spring, producing spectacular color around the lake, along with many other beautiful plantings in the area of the park known as Heath Gardens. Just across West Liberty Street lies the Bland Gardens, which has a boardwalk that extends into a natural cypress swamp. These gardens altogether make up around 150 acres of serene habitat for relaxing walks and a great natural experience.

For bird enthusiasts, the gardens provide habitat for some 122 species during the year, according to naturalist Josh Arrants. Songbirds such as the Prothonotary Warbler, Pine Warbler, Northern Parula, and Yellow-throated Warbler are common during the breeding season. In winter, the trees and shrubbery are inhabited by Ruby-crowned Kinglets, Yellow-rumped Warblers, Carolina Chickadees, and Dark-eyed Juncos. A captive population including all eight of the world's swan species likely helps attract numerous common waterfowl, including Wood Ducks, Mallards, Ring-necked Ducks, and Hooded Mergansers, and occasionally Canvasbacks and Redheads. Common herons like the Great Blue Heron and Great Egret, along with Anhingas and Double-crested Cormorants, are also present during the year.

Cypress Wetlands and Sands Beach in Port Royal, South Carolina

The town of Port Royal is located on Port Royal Island in the South Carolina Low Country, between Beaufort River on the east and Battery Creek

The cypress wetlands in Port Royal, South Carolina

Nesting egrets and Anhingas

on the west. It is a bustling, quaint seaside community, with a historic village in the center of town. This area has undergone environmentally sensitive development, preserving a unique natural environment that attracts many birds.

The cypress wetlands on Paris Avenue in Port Royal's old village might easily have been developed for commercial purposes. Instead the town has installed an amphitheater for educational programs and walking trails that are wheelchair accessible. This provides visitors with great views of nesting birds, including Anhingas, Great Blue Herons, and Great Egrets, during the breeding season. This site is well known as one of the ten best birding spots in the South Carolina Low Country. The Audubon Society has assisted with the establishment of the bird sanctu-

A wildlife shelter
corridor under
a power line

ary and nature preserve, and locals hope the site will be designated an
Audubon sanctuary.

Sands Beach, located at the confluence of the Beaufort River and Battery Creek on Port Royal Sound, features salt marsh, a sandy beach, and
a bit of scrub habitat. There is a very nice boardwalk here leading to a
forty-foot-high observation tower. In winter, waterfowl can be observed,
while in spring or summer such species as American Oystercatcher,
Clapper Rail, American Bittern, Ruddy Turnstone, and summer gulls
may be present.

Private Rural Properties

Rural properties range from individual home sites to family farms to
large-scale corporate farms and timber operations. Following are a few
examples of ways people are attracting birds to rural properties.

The Henry Farm

Frank and Cindy Henry live on a farm in the Winnabow community in
Brunswick County, North Carolina. Like many farm owners these days,
Frank and Cindy rent the farmland to a local farmer. Frank runs a busi-
ness and Cindy is a retired educator.

While they do not actively farm the land, Frank plants several parcels
with millets, sorghum, or sunflowers as food patches for birds and other
wildlife. In addition, he has planted strips of native grasses and wildflow-

A Chipping
Sparrow

Wild Turkeys in
a food plot

ers around the perimeter of the fields and has established several hedge-rows of shrubs and trees across the farm that provide food and cover for local wildlife.

There are several Purple Martin houses and more than forty bird-houses along the farm's roads and shelterbelts. Each year several Eastern Bluebirds raise their families here, and Carolina Chickadees and Tufted Titmice also nest in the boxes. In recent years Wild Turkeys have returned to the farm, and they are regularly seen in the corn and soybean fields. They also take advantage of the food plots, along with small seed-eating birds such as Chipping Sparrows, Indigo Buntings, and Blue Grosbeaks. White Ibis and Cattle Egrets, which nest in colonies on the nearby Cape Fear River, regularly forage in the fields in spring and early summer.

The Henry farm borders Town Creek, a coastal blackwater stream, on the north, and small streams run along the eastern and western edges of the farm. Town Creek is home to beavers, and Wood Ducks and Prothonotary Warblers are present there each summer. The Henrys have provided nest boxes for both species.

Town Creek at the
north boundary of
the Henry farm

A male
Prothonotary
Warbler in a
nest box

A field of
sunflowers

The Hinson Farm

The Hinson farm, owned by W. A. Hinson Jr., is located in Marlboro
County near Clio, South Carolina. This third-generation farm encompasses more than 2,000 acres of actively cultivated fields, pine woodlands, and mixed hardwood forests. Wetlands such as ponds, streams,
and beaver sloughs are also part of this beautiful farm landscape. The
primary crops grown on this property are cotton, soybeans, corn, and
tobacco.

Mr. Hinson also plants several acres of sunflowers to attract Mourning Doves, which are hunted each fall. The sunflowers are not harvested
and are left standing all winter to provide food for the birds even in the
snow. Mr. Hinson has observed an unusual feeding behavior by Mourning Doves: they tend to land on the sunflower heads to extract the seeds
instead of feeding on the ground. The sunflowers also attract many other
bird species, including the following:

American Crow
American Goldfinch
Blue Grosbeak
Brown-headed Cowbird
Carolina Chickadee

Chipping Sparrow
Eastern Phoebe
House Finch
Indigo Bunting
Northern Cardinal
Savannah Sparrow
Song Sparrow
Tufted Titmouse
Wild Turkey

A male Blue
Grosbeak on
a sunflower

The Hendrix Farm

Ramona and Jim Hendrix live in the community of Peachtree near the town of Murphy in far western North Carolina. Both are active birders and have made their farm attractive to a variety of birds. They have several feeders located where they can enjoy the birds from their windows. Birdhouses attract Eastern Bluebirds, Carolina Chickadees, Tufted Titmice, Tree Swallows, and Purple Martins. Cardinals and Song Sparrows nest in the foundation shrubbery around their home and dine at their feeders, along with American Goldfinches, Mourning Doves, and a variety of other species.

The Hendrixes let natural vegetation grow high in their ditch banks

A hummingbird
feeder on the
Hendrixes'
front porch

and field edges to provide both feeding and nesting habitat for a variety of local birds, including Red-winged Blackbirds and Indigo Buntings. Meadowlarks share the pastures with their cattle. Blue Jays and others share the fruit of their apple orchard. The Hendrix home and its surroundings are a great example of how families can share their living space with a variety of bird species.

Perhaps the most important action that landowners can take to attract and support birdlife is to maintain as many of the natural habitats associated with their properties as possible. Natural habitats are being lost at an alarming rate, and without appropriate habitat many wildlife species will vanish.

Feeders in the
Hendrixes'
front yard

A hayfield with
natural cover along
a ditch bank

Suburban Homes

The Emery Home

The Emerys' backyard, with plants and feeders

Donna and Dave Emery live in the community of Scotts Hill, just north of Wilmington, North Carolina. Donna is a retired educator and Dave a retired horticulturist. They are avid gardeners and backyard bird-watchers. They maintain a variety of feeders and birdbaths, and their yard is almost always crowded with birds. They have hummingbirds all year, and every winter their yard is home to several Baltimore Orioles in addition to more common local birds, such as American Goldfinches, Gray Catbirds, Ruby-crowned Kinglets, and White-throated Sparrows. During the winters of 2017–18 and 2018–19 a Western Tanager was also a regular visitor to their feeders.

In addition to providing feeders, the Emerys grow native plants such as salvia, trumpet vine, and zinnias, which provide natural food for their hummingbirds. American beautyberry, American holly, dogwood, several species of oaks, and wax myrtle provide food for their fruit- and seed-eating birds.

The Emerys also have allowed portions of their yard to develop into natural shrub thicket and forest, which provide escape cover and nesting habitats as well as natural food sources for their birds.

OPPOSITE
A male Indigo Bunting

Ways to Prevent Bird-Window Collisions

It is estimated that over one billion birds are killed by striking windows each year. There are two major causes of these bird-window collisions. During daylight hours birds may see reflections of plants in windows or actual potted plants inside. At night migratory birds may be attracted by the lights in your home. In both cases the birds attempt to fly through what they see as an open space and strike the glass.

Methods to reduce bird-window collisions range from simple and inexpensive to more complex and costly. All of these efforts are designed to make windows more obvious to birds and thus reduce the number of strikes.

The simpler techniques are often used by homeowners as well as in commercial buildings with lots of glass. The American Bird Conservancy (ABC) works in collaboration with a company called CollidEscape to promote the use of an adhesive film that's applied to the outside of window glass. This adhesive film is sold in the form of ¾"-wide tape, figures of birds, and various patterns, such as small circles and squares. If the tape is applied in vertical strips, the strips should be placed 4" inches apart. If it's applied in horizontal strips, the strips should be 2" apart. The tape is very durable and can last up to four years.

A very simple strategy that seems to help in reducing collisions is to simply rub a bar of soap in a line across the outside of the window. Another inexpensive method is to use a yellow highlighter to draw horizontal or vertical lines across the inside of a window. Horizontal lines should be 2" apart; vertical lines should be 4" apart. Some homeowners have hung strands of monofilament fishing line 4" to 6" apart from the top of windows, with a paper clip at the bottom of each line. This allows for some side-to-side movement of the lines. Another possibility is the use of Acopian BirdSavers (birdsavers.com), which are parachute cords suspended vertically from the top of a window, 4" apart. You can also install removable window screens during migration and then store them the rest of the year. Another option is to hang lace curtains that are attractive and let in plenty of light.

Several companies produce decals that may be applied to the outside of windows. Some are black and often in hawk shapes. A hawk

A cutout of a hawk silhouette attached to a window

shape cut from a thin piece of plywood and hung inside a window will have a similar effect. Other decals are designed to be less obvious to humans but reflect ultraviolet light, making them stand out for birds.

Each year Toronto experiences heavy bird mortality because of bird-window collisions during migration. Since 2010 the city has been implementing changes that have reduced bird-window collisions and mortality, including reducing the amount of glass in new buildings, placing dot or square patterns on windows, recessing windows to reduce reflection, using shutters or sun shades to hide glass, and simply switching off lights at night.

A Western Tanager

A Red-bellied
Woodpecker at
a suet feeder

Feeders and a birdbath seen from our family room window

One of our small backyard ponds

The Parnell Home

We (Frances and Jim) have lived on a 3.5-acre heavily wooded site in Wilmington, North Carolina, since 1966. We attract a variety of woodland birds by managing the habitat and by providing food, water, and nest boxes.

A Tufted Titmouse
at a tube feeder

Our home is tucked into the woods in such a way that most of the property is forested with live oaks, laurel oaks, and loblolly pines, with an understory of wax myrtle and other native shrubs. This provides good cover and natural food sources for birds throughout the year. We've added three small ponds to provide water, and a birdbath is placed for good viewing from the family room window. In this environment even the occasional dead tree can be left standing for woodpeckers to forage for grubs and to excavate nest cavities, until the tree falls.

Case Studies

An Apartment

Folks living in the apartment complexes that are becoming such an important component of our landscapes may also be able to attract birds if feeders and baths are allowed and if apartment balconies or yards provide some vegetative cover. Pete and Phyllis Ambler place a bird feeder near a window and watch the cardinals, chickadees, and titmice come. A nectar feeder and a few nearby flowering plants attract a steady flow of hummingbirds. A simple birdbath provides water for drinking and bathing.

Nearby shrubs or trees like crape myrtles provide escape cover and will make your birds more comfortable coming to feeders and baths.

A Brightmore retirement community apartment

Special Species in the Carolinas

6

There are several species of birds that folks in the Carolinas are particularly interested in attracting to their properties. In this chapter we'll discuss the most desired species as well as those that are most likely to be attracted to Carolina yards.

American Goldfinch

American Goldfinches, sometimes called wild canaries, nest across much of the Piedmont and mountains of North Carolina and the mountains of South Carolina. American Goldfinches don't usually nest in residential yards in the suburbs or cities. They are often rather late nesters and select sites in shrubs and trees along ditches, creek banks, and field or forest edges, usually in rural settings.

At the end of the nesting season, goldfinches gather in flocks and move to their winter quarters. This may involve short-distance movements or migrations of several hundred miles. Populations in the Carolinas swell in winter, and many of the flocks move into the Coastal Plain, where they are scarce or absent in summer.

Goldfinches primarily eat seeds during fall and winter, and they readily visit feeders in relatively open settings. They seldom visit feeders in heavily wooded yards. While they will accept a variety of foods, nyjer (*Guizotia abyssinica*), often referred to as thistle, appears to be a favorite, and many people erect special thistle feeders just to provide food for these spectacular birds. Goldfinches will also feed readily on black oil sunflower seeds, and in the fall they'll flock to sunflower plantings where the flower heads have been allowed to go to seed.

During spring and summer male goldfinches are brilliant in their breeding plumage. In autumn, however, the males molt to a more subdued color and resemble females and immature birds. In the Coastal Plain, folks may never see males in their breeding plumage, as the birds often move back to the nesting areas before they molt again to breeding colors in late winter.

A male American Goldfinch

Species Most Commonly Attracted to Carolina Yards

American Goldfinch
American Robin
Blue Grosbeak
Brown-headed Nuthatch
Brown Thrasher
Carolina Chickadee
Carolina Wren
Cedar Waxwing
Chipping Sparrow
Downy Woodpecker
Eastern Bluebird

Great-crested Flycatcher
House Finch
Mourning Dove
Northern Cardinal
Northern Mockingbird
Pine Warbler
Red-bellied Woodpecker
Ruby-throated Hummingbird
Song Sparrow
Tufted Titmouse
White-breasted Nuthatch
White-throated Sparrow

American Robin

Robins are often heralded as harbingers of spring, and in more northern states that may be true, but in the coastal Carolinas, robins are present throughout the winter—often in large numbers. In the Coastal Plain, robins feed in large flocks in bare farm fields all winter, and sometimes they roost in large, mixed-species aggregations with Red-winged and other blackbirds. When spring comes, most move northward to nest in the country and the suburbs across the northernmost states and Canada.

Robins nest across most of the Piedmont and in the lower elevations of our mountains, and in recent years their nesting range has been spreading east and south. Robins build open nests of mud and plant material, often on a horizontal limb of a suburban shade tree. They are persistent singers with a melodious song, though it's not as pretty as similar songs from their cousin the Wood Thrush.

Robins do not usually visit feeders but will readily probe for insects and worms on your lawn or in your garden. They may even follow you as you dig in your garden to glean the worms that you turn up. They will also compete with Cedar Waxwings for your holly and pyracantha berries in late winter.

LEFT
A female American Goldfinch

ABOVE
An American Robin

OPPOSITE
A Carolina Wren

A male
Baltimore Oriole

A female
Baltimore Oriole

Baltimore Oriole

In the Carolinas, Baltimore Orioles nest only in the northwestern corner of North Carolina. Here they can be found in summer primarily in the riverine forests bordering such mountain streams as the New River. Over most of the Carolinas they are transient, passing through during migration in spring and fall. However, a few will overwinter in the Carolinas, especially along the coast. Here they are attracted to feeders providing sweet treats such as grape jelly and oranges. Feeders should be established early in the fall, and if the orioles find them, and if the surrounding habitat provides for their needs, these spectacular birds may stay for the winter. As with all winter feeding, once you have attracted birds you should commit to maintaining the feeder until spring.

Carolina Chickadee and Tufted Titmouse

If your neighborhood has lots of trees and well-developed shrubbery anywhere in the Carolinas, you will likely have chickadees and titmice. Carolina Chickadees can be found in almost all parts of the Carolinas,

Carolina Birds That Will Nest in Birdhouses

A Brown-headed Nuthatch at a nest box

BARN OWLS usually nest in natural hollows but will nest in old buildings and nest boxes.

BROWN-HEADED NUTHATCHES usually excavate their own nest cavities but will use nest boxes.

CAROLINA CHICKADEES usually nest in old woodpecker cavities but will readily use nest boxes.

CAROLINA WRENS prefer a secluded niche in flower arrangement, a garage shelf, or an old tin can, but will occasionally use a nest box.

EASTERN BLUEBIRDS usually nest in abandoned woodpecker cavities but will readily accept nest boxes.

EASTERN SCREECH OWLS usually nest in natural cavities but will readily utilize Wood Duck boxes.

GREAT-CRESTED FLYCATCHERS usually nest in abandoned woodpecker cavities but will occasionally nest in a newspaper box and will also accept nest boxes.

HOODED MERGANSERS usually nest in natural cavities but will occasionally nest in a Wood Duck box.

HOUSE WRENS usually nest in abandoned woodpecker cavities but will readily accept nest boxes.

PROTHONOTARY WARBLERS usually nest in abandoned woodpecker cavities but will readily accept nest boxes.

PURPLE MARTINS occasionally will nest in abandoned woodpecker cavities, but most now nest in martin houses or gourds.

RED-BELLIED WOODPECKERS usually excavate their own cavities in dead trees but will occasionally accept a nest box.

TREE SWALLOWS usually nest in abandoned woodpecker cavities but will readily accept nest boxes.

TUFTED TITMICE usually nest in abandoned woodpecker cavities but will readily accept nest boxes.

WOOD DUCKS usually nest in natural cavities but will readily utilize nest boxes.

RIGHT
A Carolina
Chickadee

BELOW
A Tufted Titmouse

A Carolina Wren

A Carolina Wren
carrying food to
nestlings in a
nest on a front
door wreath

but folks living at very high altitudes in western North Carolina may see Black-capped Chickadees instead.

Carolina Chickadees and Tufted Titmice relish black oil sunflower seeds, and a feeder stocked with this staple will almost certainly attract a steady stream of birds of both species. They will also visit suet feeders, especially in cold weather.

Carolina Chickadees and Tufted Titmice are cavity nesters, and the box that you place for Eastern Bluebirds will likely attract these birds as well. If you are trying to attract Eastern Bluebirds and get chickadees or titmice instead, simply place another nest box or two nearby and perhaps you will be able to enjoy all three species nesting in your yard.

Carolina Wren

The Carolina Wren is the state bird of South Carolina, and most country and suburban homes in the Carolinas come with a pair of Carolina wrens. (We are not sure whether builders are required to provide a pair with each new home or the wrens have scouts constantly on the lookout for new homes being constructed.) If you live in the Carolinas and have any shrubbery in your yard, you are likely to have these wrens for neighbors. If you leave your garage door open in spring, they will likely move in and begin hauling nesting material from the yard to some niche on a

ABOVE
A Cedar Waxwing
with waxy feather
tips displayed

RIGHT
A Cedar Waxwing
feeding on yaupon
holly berries

shelf, or even to an upturned ball cap or tin can. Don't bother to put up a birdhouse for them: they prefer your garage, and if you manage to shut them out, they will likely nest in a wreath on your door, beneath your gas grill, in your boat, or in some other secluded niche.

Carolina Wrens primarily eat insects and will not regularly come to seed feeders. They will, however, visit your suet feeders, and will pay for their food with song through all but the coldest part of the year.

Cedar Waxwing

Cedar Waxwings are transient across much of the Carolinas, passing northward in late winter and early spring. In the upper Piedmont and the mountains, they become summer residents. Here they are sporadic nesters and do not come to feeders. A pair may occasionally nest in a yard with well-developed conifers such as hemlock or spruce.

For most of us, Cedar Waxwings are a mixed blessing. They are attractive birds, and when they arrive, they usually do so in numbers. The red waxy tips on their secondary wing feathers are quite unique: only Cedar Waxwings and their northern relative the Bohemian Waxwing have these structures, whose function is not fully known.

LEFT
A female Eastern
Bluebird at a nest
box entrance

ABOVE
A male Eastern
Bluebird bringing
food to nestlings

But when they visit our yards, it is usually to gobble up all of the holly and pyracantha berries, leaving none for the resident Northern Mockingbirds or flocks of American Robins, which also relish the berries. It may take flocks of Cedar Waxwings only a few minutes or a day or two to clean up all of the berries, and then the flock is off to a neighbor's yard, not to visit again until next year.

Eastern Bluebird

The Eastern Bluebird is the species that Carolinians seem to want most to attract to their property. While bluebirds will readily accept birdhouses in appropriate habitats, they are not regular visitors to most feeders. If you wish to attract bluebirds to nest in your yard, the most important factor is habitat. Bluebirds like relatively open areas for nesting. If your yard is heavily wooded, your efforts will likely fail. They prefer scattered trees and open lawns. If you can provide this type of habitat—and it is typical of many suburban developments—they may accept your offer of a nest box. In rural environments bluebirds will often nest in boxes placed along farm roads or field borders. The same rules apply here; the area needs to be relatively open.

The population of Eastern Bluebirds declined dramatically in the 1960s with the loss of naturally existing habitat and natural nest cavities. By the early 1970s the concept of bluebird trails was introduced, and Boy Scout troops, garden clubs, and others began to place rows of bluebird houses along roadsides, golf courses, and other appropriate places. This has been an important factor in increasing the number of Eastern Bluebirds, and while populations have rebounded, there is still a strong need for bluebird houses because natural cavities continue to be lost.

Nest boxes can be simple or elaborate. What's important is that the nest hole is one and a half inches in diameter, the box is about five to six feet above the ground, it faces the open portion of your yard, and it's not close to thick shrubbery or trees. Nest boxes less than one hundred yards apart are not likely to be used by bluebirds but may well be occupied by Carolina Chickadees or Tufted Titmice.

For many years we thought that Eastern Bluebirds could not be regularly attracted to feeders because they primarily eat insects and fruit, not seeds or suet. However, many years ago Jack Finch (who, you may remember from this book's introduction, founded the nonprofit group Homes for Bluebirds) had success attracting bluebirds to feeders stocked with dogwood berries. He gathered the ripe berries in late summer and, we believe, refrigerated them until used. But that process is labor intensive and probably not doable for most homeowners.

A newer trend is to provide mealworms on a shelf feeder. Meal-

worms can be purchased at some bird supply stores, and apparently bluebirds relish them.

A major problem for Eastern Bluebirds is competition for nest boxes by European Starlings and, to a lesser degree, House Sparrows. A one-and-a-half-inch opening in a nest box will keep out starlings while admitting bluebirds, but there is no good solution for keeping out House Sparrows. If your birdhouse is near a wooded area, another problem is flying squirrels. These critters can easily enter the one-and-a-half-inch hole and may take over a nest box.

Eastern Bluebird houses are also often occupied by native backyard birds such as Carolina Chickadees and Tufted Titmice. The solution here is to place several boxes around the yard. While bluebirds will not normally nest in close proximity to other bluebirds (boxes on a bluebird trail should be at least one hundred feet apart), multiple boxes will help to ensure that all of the local cavity-nesting species find a suitable nest box. That way you can enjoy the bluebirds as well as chickadees, titmice, and others. Be sure to clean out the boxes at the end of the nesting season to help to eliminate parasites that may overwinter in the old nest material.

Eastern Screech Owl

Most suburban folks will not wish to attract this small owl to their property because the diet of Eastern Screech Owls includes small birds. On

LEFT
Eastern Screech Owl chicks peering from a nest box

ABOVE
A gray-phase Eastern Screech Owl roosting in a natural cavity

A male Eastern Towhee

larger properties, however, these owls add to the diversity of birdlife, and their trills are an intriguing part of a spring evening.

Eastern Screech Owls are residents of forested habitats across much of the Carolinas, excepting the higher mountains. They are seldom seen, but their trilling calls are unique and interesting. Eastern Screech Owls come in two color phases, red and gray, and both color phases may occur in a single brood.

Screech owls usually roost and nest in old woodpecker holes or in natural cavities in living or dead trees. They will, however, readily accept houses built for Wood Ducks, especially if the houses are placed in upland woodlands. (For details on boxes for Wood Ducks and screech owls, see the sidebar later in this chapter.)

We have had Eastern Screech Owls roosting and nesting in Wood Duck boxes on our property in Wilmington several times over the past years. The gray-phase owl in the photo on the previous page roosted in a hollow tree section cut from a downed tree and then strapped to a live tree.

Eastern Towhee

Eastern Towhees are common permanent residents across much of the Carolinas. They prefer thick forest edges but will sometimes move into suburban yards where there is an abundance of thick shrubbery. They

A Birdhouse for Common Backyard Birds

A bluebird nest box

Brown-headed Nuthatch
Carolina Chickadee
Eastern Bluebird
House Wren
Prothonotary Warbler
Tree Swallow
Tufted Titmouse

Eastern Bluebird houses come in a wide variety of forms, from plain to fancy, but all will suffice so long as the basic size parameters are met. The plans here are for a Jack Finch–designed house, and it's one of the best designs that we have seen. Bluebirds will readily use it, and it is easy to construct, clean, and repair.

The entrance hole should be 1½″ in diameter. This will allow bluebirds in and keep starlings out. For Brown-headed Nuthatches, reduce the entrance hole diameter to 1⅛″. A metal (copper or aluminum) hole guard is an important addition because it will prevent woodpeckers and squirrels from enlarging the entrance hole.

Here are the basic plans for the box, using ¾″ stock:

BACK: 5½″ by 16″
SIDES: 4″ by 10″ in back, 4″ by 9″ in front
FRONT: 5½″ by 9″
BOTTOM: 4″ by 4″
TOP: 6½″ by 7″
ENTRANCE HOLE: 1½″ diameter;
      1⅛″ for Brown-headed Nuthatch

A nest box with an open front

Always arrange for the front to tilt open so that the box can be cleaned at the end of the season. Attaching the front with two opposing screws near the top of the panel will allow the front to swing open.

Mount the box on a post 5′ to 6′ above the ground. Where snakes or squirrels are present, a predator guard is a very good idea.

may also nest in suburban yards where thick cover is present, usually placing their nests within a few feet of the ground.

Eastern Towhees seldom visit elevated feeders, but they will readily feed on cracked corn or millet placed on the ground near escape cover.

House Wren

House Wrens are backyard-nesting birds throughout the lower-to-mid elevations in the mountains of the Carolinas. Nesting is less widespread in the Piedmont and even more sporadic in the Coastal Plain. They are, however, widespread winter residents of thick, brushy habitats in the Coastal Plain.

House Wrens prefer yards with lots of dense shrubbery. They will readily accept houses built for Eastern Bluebirds and will even nest in martin gourds on occasion. Their nest is a bulky affair, often completely filling the birdhouse. House Wrens eat a wide variety of small insects, spiders, and other invertebrates.

This small, rather nondescript wren is a persistent singer, and its song is quite distinct from that of the more widespread and common Carolina Wren. This species is sometimes polyandrous. A paired female may leave a newly hatched brood of chicks to be fed by the male and move into the territory of another male to begin a new family.

A female
Ruby-throated
Hummingbird at
a Turk's cap flower

Hummingbirds

The Ruby-throated Hummingbird is our native summer resident hummingbird. This is the hummingbird species that you will see visiting your flower beds in summer and, if you are very lucky, placing a tiny cup-shaped nest on a tree limb in your yard.

Ruby-throats are attracted by flowers, especially those that are red, produce good amounts of nectar, and have easily accessible nectar. Examples include lobelias, native coral honeysuckle, trumpet vine, and salvia.

Hummingbirds will also visit feeders that provide a sugar-water substitute for natural nectar. While there are many feeder types, the old standby shown on the next page is still probably the best bet. You can purchase premixed nectar substitutes, but four heaping teaspoons of sugar dissolved in a cup of water will work just fine. Hummingbird feeders should be cleaned at least once a week and more often in hot weather. Dispose of any unused nectar mix at this time. Use very hot water, soap, and a bottle brush to remove any fungus or bacteria that may be growing

Ruby-throated
Hummingbirds
crowding a feeder

in the feeder, and then add fresh nectar. It is usually not necessary to use bleach to clean a hummingbird feeder, unless it's heavily infected with mold. If you do use bleach, be sure to rinse the feeder thoroughly before refilling it with nectar mix. Place your feeder near a window where you can enjoy the birds as they feed. Hummers can be belligerent at feeders, and more than one feeder may be needed to keep everybody happy.

In recent years bird-watchers have discovered that some species of hummingbirds that are normally found in the western United States, such as the Rufous Hummingbird, visit the Carolinas in fall and winter. In the early years of feeding hummingbirds, we were told to take down our hummingbird feeders when the weather began to cool in the fall to encourage the hummers to migrate and not remain into the winter. Now that we know that several species of western hummers, as well as some Ruby-throated Hummingbirds, may be present in winter—even in areas with no feeders—we have begun leaving our hummingbird feeders out and filled all winter. Many folks, especially along the coast, now have one or more species of hummers at their feeders all winter.

If you decide to leave your hummingbird feeder out in the fall and winter, there are several things that you need to do. First, and most important, you need to commit to keeping the feeder filled all winter. Do not encourage birds to stay and then stop feeding them in midwinter! Second, you must have a strategy for keeping the contents of the feeder from freezing during cold weather. You can take the feeder into the

A male Northern Bobwhite, calling

house when the sun goes down and, on days when temperatures are not expected to stay below freezing, take it back outside in the morning. You can also devise a feeder heater to keep the feeder from freezing. We mount a feeder on our back deck early in the fall and let the hummers get used to its location. When cold weather comes, we place a lamp with a 100-watt incandescent bulb in a large tin can with a hole in the top and place the can just below the feeder. We turn the lamp on at dusk, and it keeps the liquid in the feeder from freezing during most of the winter. When there is a winter-resident hummer, it will usually be at the feeder shortly after daylight, and a warm breakfast is likely appreciated.

Northern Bobwhite

The recent story of the bobwhite in the Carolinas is not a happy one. Once common in farmland and the open pine woodlands of the Sand-hills and Coastal Plain, bobwhites are now scarce and scattered. While the reasons for their decline are not clear, it is very likely that it's due to a combination of factors, including changes in farming practices, the de-cline of open longleaf pine forests, and loss of habitat to development.

ABOVE
A molting female
Northern Cardinal

RIGHT
A female Northern
Cardinal at a nest

The bobwhite is still out there, and you may still hear the "bobwhite" call of the male upon occasion, but not nearly so often as in the past.

Since the bobwhite is classified as a game bird, wildlife agencies in both Carolinas are working to generate a comeback of this popular resident. Perhaps we will see a success story similar to that of the Wild Turkey someday.

Attracting bobwhites is probably beyond the capability of most folks in the suburbs, but there is still hope in rural areas. What can rural landowners do today to enhance their property for bobwhites? The best advice is probably to think back to what farms looked like in the 1950s, before megafarms and the heavy use of herbicides became the norm. Bobwhites flourished on small farms with weedy, overgrown ditch banks and field edges. There was good escape and nesting cover and lots of food in the form of native grass and weed seeds. Wildlife professionals are still working to develop detailed recommendations for attracting bobwhites, but if you are serious about enticing bobwhites to your property or enhancing conditions for birds already present, be sure to read the fact sheet from the South Carolina Department of Natural Resources on bobwhites (https://www.clemson.edu/extension/scaged/scffa/career-development-events/files/wildlife/SC-DNR-QuailGuide.pdf).

Northern Cardinal

The Northern Cardinal is the state bird of North Carolina, and cardinals are widespread in both Carolinas from the coast to the middle altitudes in the mountains.

Northern Cardinals are birds of woodlands and field edges, and many suburbs closely resemble this natural habitat. Thus, Northern Car-

dinals are common around homes from farms to city suburbs. If there are scattered trees and well-developed shrubbery, cardinals are likely to be present.

Northern Cardinals primarily eat seeds and will become regular customers at feeders stocked with either black oil or striped sunflower seeds. They will also visit suet feeders.

They build their cup-shaped nests in either dense shrubbery or low trees, usually within a few feet of the ground. Foundation plantings such as azaleas and hollies provide suitable habitat, and cardinals will often nest just outside a window.

Cardinals often completely molt the feathers on their head in July. This gives rise to strange-looking bald-headed birds for a few days, until new feathers emerge.

Northern Mockingbird

The Northern Mockingbird is a common permanent resident of the Carolinas from the coast to the lower sections of the mountains. Its

A Northern
Mockingbird
eating a
beautyberry

natural habitat is the edge between forest and open areas, but it has found cities and suburbs to be quite suitable substitutes. If you live in the woods you will not likely have mockingbirds in your yard, but most suburbs, with their scattered trees, dense foundation plantings of evergreen shrubs, and open lawns, are readily occupied.

Northern Mockingbirds will build their nests in your shrubbery and raise their families in your yards. They are persistent songsters and will sing throughout the day and night, sometimes to the chagrin of light sleepers.

These mockingbirds primarily eat insects and fruit and will not usually visit feeders stocked with seeds, but they will sometimes visit a suet feeder. Berry-producing plants such as hollies, pyracantha, and

beautyberry will provide good food sources for mockingbirds as well as other fruit-eating species.

LEFT
An Osprey landing on a nest in a cypress tree

ABOVE
An adult Osprey

Osprey

Ospreys are one of the most widespread of the world's raptors, found on all continents except Antarctica. In the United States, Ospreys have suffered greatly in the past because of heavy use of the pesticide DDT. The Carolinas, however, did not see the magnitude of decline seen in other regions, and Ospreys have remained relatively common and widespread here.

Ospreys were once found primarily along the coast, but the advent of large reservoirs across the Carolinas has resulted in the spread of the species across both states. Ospreys are almost exclusively fish eaters and generally nest over or very near water. Nests are usually bulky affairs placed in living or dead trees, from just a few feet above the water to the treetops. Ospreys will also build on structures such as power poles, channel markers, and ball field light poles.

Many waterfront property owners would like to attract Ospreys to nest on or adjacent to their property. Nest platforms placed in relatively open and undisturbed areas with easy access for large flying birds will sometimes be used by Ospreys. Nest platforms do not have to be over water, but those that are have a greater likelihood of being used. Nest

An Osprey Nest Platform

Ospreys normally build their bulky nests in living or dead trees over water or along the perimeter of large bodies of water. They will also use artificial structures such as channel markers or nesting platforms. There are a variety of plans for nesting platforms on the internet, but the one recommended by the Conserve Wildlife Foundation of New Jersey appears to be a good basic design. It calls for a 3'-by-3' platform constructed of 2"-by-8" and 2"-by-6" boards. The nest platform should be attached to the top of a 16'-long 6"-by-6" treated pole. Two perches should be added, and a predator guard should be placed below the nest to prevent raccoons from reaching the eggs.

platforms can be constructed in living trees, or they can be placed atop poles sunk into the ground.

Painted Bunting

The Painted Bunting is one of the Carolinas' most spectacular birds. Everybody would love to have them living in their yard. What can you do to attract them? Well, in North Carolina, preferably you'd live on the coast south of Morehead City: Painted Buntings spend the summer on the immediate coast from about Morehead City southward. If you cannot smell the salt marsh from your yard, then you probably will not attract Painted Buntings no matter what you do. But in South Carolina they begin to move inland, at least as far as Florence and Hartsville.

Painted Buntings like white proso millet, a food not readily eaten by most other backyard birds. A tube feeder filled with this millet in the proper habitat will likely attract these spectacular birds. Most depart southward in autumn, but an occasional bird will overwinter here. Painted Buntings will also regularly visit birdbaths in or adjacent to their chosen habitats, so watch for them there.

This species is having a difficult time, and East Coast populations appear to be declining. Most Painted Buntings winter in the northern Caribbean, southern Mexico, and Central America, where they are often sought for the caged-bird market. Trapping and habitat loss are likely involved in their decline.

Prothonotary Warbler

The Prothonotary Warbler is a summer resident of wooded swamps and stream banks across the Carolinas, from the coast into the Piedmont. These insectivorous birds seldom come to feeders, but they will occasionally visit a suet feeder.

Prothonotary Warblers usually nest in old woodpecker cavities, or in natural cavities or partially enclosed niches in the bark of trees over water. However, if you live next to a swamp, floodplain, wooded lakefront, or wooded stream, you may be able to attract this bird with the placement of a birdhouse. They will accept typical bluebird houses placed over water or near streams or flooded ponds. They will even occasionally nest in typical suburban yards if water is nearby.

Purple Martin

Purple Martins are summer residents over much of the Carolinas. All, or nearly all, Purple Martins now nest in artificial housing, either gourds or multicompartment houses. Apparently they originally nested in old woodpecker holes in trees, and a few may still do so.

To attract Purple Martins, you must have an open area for the nest boxes. They usually won't nest where there is much cover from trees or shrubs nearby. Open areas next to agricultural fields, large open yards, and open areas adjacent to lakes or marshes are most likely to attract nesting birds. Be aware, however, that some important factors seem to be understood only by the martins—some housing complexes in what

appear to be ideal conditions will go unused. Martins may also use a housing complex for several years and then, for no apparent reason, fail to return.

Purple Martins are gregarious birds that often nest in colonies consisting of many pairs. They will readily nest in close groupings, which makes the modern multiapartment birdhouses perfect for martins. There is much discussion among martin lovers about the best kinds of housing complexes. Apartment houses such as the one above have several advantages. One pole and one housing complex provides nest apartments for several pairs of birds. Higher-quality units are long lasting and are relatively easy to clean at the end of the nesting season. They are, however, also attractive to European Starlings, and these aggressive birds often end up the primary owners of such housing complexes.

Natural gourds, hung so that they sway in the wind, are also readily used by martins, and they do not seem so readily used by starlings. However, they have a relatively short life and must be either replaced after a few years or taken down at the end of each nesting season, carefully painted, and stored out of the weather. Recently, plastic gourds have appeared on the market. They appear to have the same advantages of the natural gourds in that the martins like them and the starlings do not, and they are much more weather resistant than the natural gourds. Still, all martin houses should be cleaned at the end of the nesting season, and it is a good idea to store all gourds out of the weather for the winter.

LEFT
A male Purple Martin at a natural gourd

ABOVE, TOP
Painted gourds and multiapartment houses for Purple Martins

ABOVE, BOTTOM
Purple Martins on a commercially produced multiple-unit house

Purple Martin Housing

NATURAL GOURDS:

- Do not last long
- Are less likely to be occupied by starlings
- Offer better protection from avian predators

PLASTIC GOURDS:

- Are weather resistant and long lasting
- Are less likely to be occupied by starlings
- Offer better protection from avian predators

MULTIAPARTMENT HOUSES:

- Are weather resistant and long lasting
- House multiple pairs of birds
- Are more likely to be occupied by starlings
- Leave chicks more vulnerable
  to avian predators

An artificial gourd
nest hung on wire

TOP
A Purple Martin
on a gourd

BOTTOM
A multiapartment
house with martins

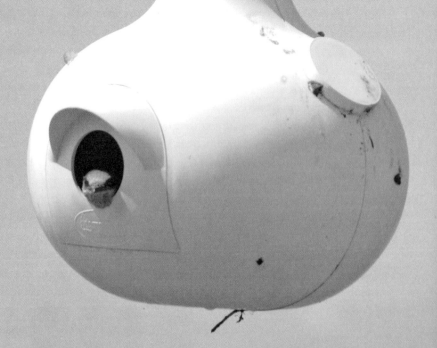

One complex of plastic gourds and apartment-style houses in Hyde County, North Carolina, is used by martins each year. The owner regularly has to evict starlings from the apartments but has little trouble with them in the gourds. He takes down the gourds as soon as the martins have completed nesting and all of the chicks have fledged, usually in late July. He removes the old nests from the gourds and stores the gourds for the winter. In early March he restrings the gourds in time for the arrival of the first martin scouts.

Another benefit of the gourds is that chicks in a gourd seem to be less vulnerable to predation by Great Horned Owls. The owner of the complex has watched Great Horned Owls alight at gourds and try to reach the chicks inside, but the swinging motion of the gourds usually prevents the owl from taking chicks. Another friend has seen hawks snatch chicks from individual units in the multicompartment houses on more than one occasion.

A female Rose-breasted Grosbeak

Rose-Breasted Grosbeak

In most of the Carolinas the Rose-breasted Grosbeak is transient, passing through on its journey north in spring and back through the Caro-

LEFT
An adult Song
Sparrow

ABOVE
A female Song
Sparrow on a nest

linas on its way south in autumn. In the mountains, however, this striking bird is a summer resident of forests above 3,000 feet. It sometimes raises its broods of chicks in heavily wooded yards.

Male Rose-breasted Grosbeaks have a song much like that of a robin but more melodious—it's sometimes described as a robin with voice training.

Rose-breasted Grosbeaks eat a variety of foods, including seeds, berries, and insects. They will come to feeders when sunflower seeds are offered, and migrating birds may occasionally stop at a feeder outside of their summer mountain homes.

Song Sparrow

Song Sparrows have an interesting distribution pattern in the Carolinas. They are common winter residents throughout much of the Carolinas, and there are also nesting populations in the mountains and across the northern perimeter of North Carolina. In addition, there is a breeding population along the Outer Banks of North Carolina.

In areas where Song Sparrows nest, they may be backyard birds where there is well-developed shrubbery. They may nest just outside your window in a rosebush or other dense shrub.

Outside of their nesting areas, Song Sparrows are winter residents of dense thickets along woodland edges or yards with well-developed stands of evergreen shrubs.

Song Sparrows primarily eat seeds and seldom visit elevated feeders.

OPPOSITE
A male Rose-
breasted Grosbeak

Cracked corn or millet placed on the ground may attract these sparrows, along with White-throated Sparrows and others.

Tree Swallow

In most of the Carolinas, the Tree Swallow is transient, passing through in spring and fall as it travels between nesting areas further north and wintering areas to the south. But in coastal Carolina, Tree Swallows may occur in huge flocks in winter, especially around coastal lakes, such as Lake Mattamuskeet in northeastern North Carolina, and over coastal marshes and fallow farm fields. They may also forage over farm ponds and the shallow impoundments created to attract waterfowl.

This species is also expanding its range southward and eastward, and it now nests at scattered locations in the Piedmont and Coastal Plain of North Carolina. In the northwestern corner of North Carolina, tree swallows have begun to stay through the summer, and here they will readily forsake their traditional old woodpecker holes for birdhouses. Houses designed for bluebirds appear to be quite suitable. If you have bluebird boxes out at locations near large bodies of water, watch for this species to move in. They consume large numbers of flying insects and should be welcomed everywhere.

Waterfowl

Attracting large numbers of wintering waterfowl requires enough space for a pond or impoundment and is thus usually accomplished in farm country. In recent years, though, the increase in the number of retention ponds in development projects in cities has certainly aided in the resur-

gence of Canada Goose populations. Such ponds may also occasionally attract ducks and mergansers.

In recent years both hunters and folks who just enjoy having waterfowl nearby have begun to construct shallow impoundments varying in size from an acre or so to many acres. These are drained in late winter and usually planted in crops such as corn, millet, or soybeans. Then in autumn, the standing mature crops are flooded with a few inches of water to provide easy access for dabbling ducks such as Mallards and Northern Pintails. Impoundments appear to be most successful when they're near a major waterfowl wintering area such as a wildlife refuge, large reservoir, or wooded swamp.

Shallow impoundments will also attract and provide feeding opportunities for wading birds such as herons, egrets, and ibis. They may also attract shorebirds during spring and fall migrations, if very shallow water conditions or mudflats coincide with migratory passages. If possible, keep water in the impoundments after the waterfowl hunting season ends to allow the birds to continue to feed until they depart for nesting grounds further north.

Beaver ponds also attract waterfowl, and if they remain undisturbed, you will certainly get Wood Ducks and other dabbling ducks as winter visitors, and the Wood Ducks will likely remain to nest.

White-Throated Sparrow

White-throated Sparrows are winter residents throughout much of the Carolinas. These are thicket-loving birds often found in dense areas along woodland edges. They will, however, overwinter in yards where there is dense cover provided by well-developed shrubbery.

White-throated Sparrows generally feed on the ground and seldom visit elevated feeders. They primarily eat seeds, and wintering flocks will often feed on cracked corn or millet placed on the ground near dense escape cover. As spring approaches white-throats often begin to sing their "Old Sam Peabody" songs prior to departing for nesting grounds across Canada.

Wild Turkey

The comeback of the Wild Turkey is one of the real wildlife management successes of recent years. When we were growing up in the Coastal Plain of South Carolina in the 1940s and 1950s, we heard of Wild Turkeys in remote places like the Great Pee Dee River Swamp but never saw them in our community. At North Carolina State University in the 1960s we were taught that you had to have large areas of mature woodlands to support Wild Turkeys. We never expected to see them in small woodlots and even in the edges of towns as we see today.

Folks in most urban areas probably will not be able to attract turkeys to their yards and feeders regularly, although there was recently a photo

LEFT
A strutting male
Wild Turkey

ABOVE
Turkey hens
foraging in a
winter wheat plot

of turkeys roosting on the banister of a deck in Asheville, North Carolina. But if you live in a rural area anywhere in the Carolinas, you are very likely to have Wild Turkeys living nearby. You may be able to attract them to your property in a variety of ways.

If you have sufficient space, you may plant food plots to attract Wild Turkeys. They relish chufa (a domesticated version of nut grass), and they're very likely to use a food plot. Be warned, however, that raccoons and wild hogs also relish chufa. Before planting chufa, check with your local agricultural agent, because growing them requires special attention. Wild Turkeys will also visit food plots planted with clover and most of the other mixtures more commonly planted for deer. They may eat the crop or forage on the grasshoppers, crickets, and other insects that are usually present in such food plots.

If planting food plots is not possible, you can scatter corn along roads in the woods, field edges, and even backyards that are adjacent to woodlands, and Wild Turkeys will readily come.

Wood Duck

Wood Ducks are permanent residents of streams, lakes, and swamps from the lower reaches of our mountains to the coast. They are most abundant in the swamps of the Coastal Plain.

Wood Ducks readily come to rural areas with a pond, stream, or swamp, and they may also move into a city where ponds or lakes are present.

Wood Ducks nest in natural cavities in trees, old woodpecker holes

A Wood Duck, Hooded Merganser, or Eastern Screech Owl Box

A nest box can be constructed from ¾" stock or full 1" stock, preferably cedar, redwood, or cypress. Here are the dimensions:

TOP: 12" by 16"
BACK: 12" by 24"
FRONT: 12" by 23"
SIDES: 12" by 23" in front, 12" by 24" in back
BOTTOM: 12" by 10"
ENTRANCE HOLE: 4" in diameter

The box should be attached to a post with a predator guard, not attached to a tree. The box should be about 5' to 6' above the ground or water. Make sure that there are no nearby tree branches that would allow a squirrel to jump to the box.

It is also a good idea to mount a bluebird box on the side of the duck box, for use by Prothonotary Warblers (see page 95 for instructions on constructing a bluebird box). The bluebird dimensions will work fine, and the warblers get the benefit of the predator guard. Dr. Eugene Hester has done this for most of his Wood Duck boxes near Wendell, North Carolina, and often has Prothonotary Warblers nesting in his boxes.

While they're uncommon during the nesting season in the Carolinas, an occasional pair of Hooded Mergansers may nest in a Wood Duck box.

A Wood Duck box and Prothonotary Warbler box sharing a support pole

A pair of Wood Ducks

(if they are large enough), and birdhouses. They are hunted, and sportsmen, Boy Scouts, and others have erected many duck boxes over the years, which has helped to restore numbers of this glamorous duck to the point that it is now among the most abundant duck species in the Carolinas.

Efforts to attract Wood Ducks usually involve creating appropriate habitat if it is not already present. Perhaps the best way to describe this is to say that you need to attract beavers to your property and let them build beaver ponds. Beaver ponds make ideal nesting and feeding habitat for woodies.

If you already have water nearby, the best thing you can do is to erect housing. Wood Ducks readily accept nesting boxes placed over shallow

A Predator Guard

Begin with a 2'-by-2' or 3'-by-3' square sheet of aluminum or galvanized metal. We prefer 3' by 3'. Locate the exact center and drill a ¼" hole. Leave the sheet square or inscribe a circle and cut it out with tin snips. Cut from one edge to the center hole. Flex the metal sheet so that the cut edges overlap to form a shallow cone and clamp. Then drill two holes through both overlapping sheets and secure the guard in the cone shape with short bolts. If the guard is to be used below a nest box, enlarge the center hole with tin snips to allow it to fit around the wooden post or metal pole. Secure the guard to the post beneath the nest box.

This guard can also be used above or below a bird feeder to prevent squirrels and raccoons from reaching the feeder.

TOP
A predator guard above a feeder

MIDDLE
A raccoon, squirrel, and snake baffle on a duck box

BOTTOM
A predator guard design layout

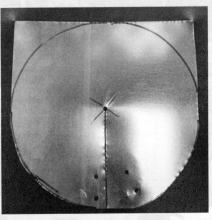

ABOVE
A Wood Duck
nest box with a
predator guard

RIGHT
A feeder over
a natural
woodland pond

water or even some distance away from water. There are records of Wood Ducks nesting near homes, in duck boxes several hundred yards from water. However, boxes near water are more likely to result in successful broods because the chicks must be taken to water upon hatching. All boxes should have predator guards to prevent snakes and raccoons from preying on the eggs and chicks. Keep the boxes well away from overhanging limbs to keep squirrels from usurping the nest box.

Wood Ducks, like most waterfowl, love corn, and a feeder that scatters corn in shallow water will prove to be a magnet if woodies are around. You can almost certainly attract woodies and other ducks by placing one of the typical feeders used by deer hunters over shallow water. A feeder and an observation blind will offer great opportunities to observe these colorful ducks at close range. The feeder shown above regularly attracts woodies each morning when it activates. It provides a great opportunity to watch the ducks and photograph their activities.

Remember, however, that feeding ducks in order to attract them for hunting (baiting) is illegal, and the practice is subject to heavy fines.

A male Wood Thrush

Check with your state agency about the specific rules regarding baiting waterfowl so that you do not violate the law or unintentionally make your neighbors into lawbreakers by establishing a feeder near property where they hunt.

Wood Thrush

The Wood Thrush is especially valued for its song. Wood Thrushes are summer residents of deciduous forests across much of the Carolinas but spend their winters in the tropics. They may nest in well-wooded suburban yards, especially in the Piedmont and lower mountains. Their numbers are declining, however, and there is much concern over the future of this species.

Wood Thrushes are not regular visitors to feeders but will occasionally visit a suet feeder. They feed primarily on invertebrates on the forest floor, but they also consume fruit such as holly berries.

Species That Sometimes Pose Problems

7

A few bird species have become problems in the Carolinas. Most of the problem species are native to other parts of the world and have been introduced into this region. Some, like the European Starling and House Sparrow, compete with native species such as the Eastern Bluebird and Purple Martin for nest sites. Others, like the Mute Swan, compete with native waterfowl. But native species can also cause problems. Some native woodpeckers occasionally damage wooden structures. The Canada Goose, once a welcomed winter resident in the Carolinas, now causes a variety of problems as a permanent resident.

In this chapter we will discuss those species that are often less than welcome. We will also look at a few non-bird species that pose problems for birds that we have attracted to our properties.

Birds

Birds interact with the other animals living in their habitats in many ways, some positive and some negative. When we attract birds and they become concentrated in and around our living spaces, we often make these interactions more visible and perhaps more frequent. Several examples are listed here, but understand that many other such interactions are part of the normal lives of birds.

Brown-Headed Cowbird

Brown-headed Cowbirds are brood parasites, laying their eggs in the nests of other small birds. A female cowbird may lay one egg in a different nest each day for several days in a season and may even remove the host's eggs. The host incubates the eggs and feeds the cowbird hatchlings, to the detriment of any host young present. Brown-headed Cowbirds may thus have a significant impact on other species' production of offspring. This is especially important for species whose populations are declining.

A female Brown-headed Cowbird

European Starlings

As their name implies, European Starlings are native to Europe. They were introduced into this country in 1890 by settlers who apparently wanted to bring a bit of their homeland to their new country. The starlings adapted to their new surroundings and spread rapidly across the continent. European Starlings are now common to abundant in both the cities and the farmlands of the Carolinas.

The problem with starlings is that they utilize the same types of nesting structures used by native Eastern Bluebirds, Purple Martins, and some woodpeckers. Starlings are aggressive when establishing nest sites and will usually outcompete native species for birdhouses. They may even toss out the eggs or small chicks of birds that have already initiated nesting.

When starlings are competing with Eastern Bluebirds, the problem can usually be solved by making sure that the opening to the bluebird house is no more than one and a half inches in diameter. This allows bluebirds to enter but keeps starlings out. This solution doesn't work for Purple Martins, however, because they, like starlings, need a larger nest opening. Some folks have found that starlings don't nest in hanging Purple Martin gourds, but this may not always work. The large multi-

apartment houses often used for Purple Martins have no protection against starlings.

European Starlings are not considered migratory birds and are not protected by federal or state laws, but check for local ordinances before disturbing their nests.

Barn Swallows

Barn Swallows are native to the Carolinas and are generally welcomed both because they're beautiful and because they eat large numbers of flying insects. Their name stems from their habit of building their nests of mud and feathers on the beams of barns. In modern times they have discovered that the supporting beams of bridges, piers, and pier houses, and the open garages beneath many hotels and condominiums are also suitable places for nests. Barn Swallows are colonial nesters, and a barn or condominium may provide nest sites for several pairs.

Nesting Barn Swallows do no damage to the nesting structure. The problem is that chicks and adults deposit their feces over the sides of the nests. Machinery or automobiles parked below may be "whitewashed" by the time the chicks are on the wing.

Barn Swallows are migratory birds and are protected by federal law. They may not be harmed or harassed, so once the nests are built the

A flock of urban Canada Geese

birds must be allowed to complete nesting. If the birds become a serious problem, it may be necessary to close off the openings to the barn or other structure before the nesting season begins. Otherwise, know that they are paying their rent by eating large numbers of flying insects, including mosquitoes.

Birds at Airports

A variety of birds have been struck by aircraft at or near airports. Waterfowl, gulls, raptors, pigeons, and doves appear to be most often involved.

Along the coast or near large inland lakes, flocks of gulls land to rest wherever there are large expanses that are free of tall vegetation. Along the coast, this includes beaches and mudflats exposed by a falling tide. Inland, gulls and Canada Geese may congregate in fallow fields or athletic fields—or on airport runways and the grasslands adjacent to them. Doves and pigeons may feed in the grasslands adjacent to runways, and such concentrations of feeding birds will likely attract hawks. This means that birds may be coming and going as planes are landing and taking off. Birds in the direct flight path of aircraft may strike the plane and even be ingested by one of the jet engines.

Airports use a variety of methods to minimize bird strikes: modifying the habitat adjacent to runways to make it less attractive to birds; playing loud sounds to frighten birds away; or using specially trained

dogs to run birds off. Spotters may also look for gatherings of birds and direct aircraft to runways where there are none.

Canada Geese

Until recently Canada Geese had a lofty reputation in the Carolinas. Folks were excited to hear flocks pass overhead in autumn during the birds' southward migration from nesting grounds in the prairies of the Dakotas and Canada. We enjoyed seeing flocks in or near refuges and feeding in harvested grain fields. When they headed northward in spring, we missed seeing and hearing these large birds.

In recent years, partly as a result of attempts to bolster local populations of winter-resident geese, Canada Geese were released in many places in the eastern states. These geese do not migrate north in spring like wild geese and find local conditions to be excellent for raising their families. The abundance of small ponds and lakes, especially the storm-water retention ponds in many new urban developments, has led to a surge in Canada Goose populations throughout the Carolinas. They have in many cases become urbanized, feeding and often nesting on or adjacent to golf courses, ball fields, and open yards. Adult geese may become very aggressive during nesting and may attack pets and even people who wander too close to nests or small goslings. As their numbers increase, they add to the fertilization of ponds and lakes and may contribute to in-

creased pollution and algae blooms. They may also become dangerous at airports when they feed in grasslands adjacent to active runways.

Wild Canada Geese are migratory birds and are protected by federal and state laws. During the nesting season, however, when only non-migratory birds are present, it may be possible to move them from areas where they have become a nuisance. At airports, trained dogs are sometimes used to chase the birds from runways. This tactic may also work at other large areas, such as golf courses. Homeowners with nuisance birds may be able to get them to move on by repeatedly flushing them. Be sure to check local laws, however, before harassing any wildlife.

Although Canada Geese certainly can be a nuisance and perhaps even a hazard, the sound and sight of a calling flock passing overhead is still as exciting in June as it is in January. In rural areas where there is adequate space for both geese and people, they remain an interesting part of the avian scene.

Grackles

Boat-tailed Grackles (along the coast) and Common Grackles (primarily inland) are native birds that can become a nuisance when they descend in large flocks on feeders and either quickly consume the available food or displace smaller birds.

Grackles are protected under the Migratory Bird Treaty Act and should not be harmed. Your best bet is to discourage them by using feeders that they cannot access. This usually means a tube feeder with a wire cage around it and openings large enough for small birds to go through but small enough to exclude grackles.

A male House
Sparrow

Hawks

When you establish a bird feeder, your goal is to attract lots of birds so that you can enjoy their presence. However, there are other avian critters that may consider your bird feeder their "bird feeder."

Cooper's Hawks and Sharp-shinned Hawks feed on other birds, and a concentration of birds around a feeder will occasionally attract a hungry hawk. You may see them perched near the feeder waiting for an unwary bird to approach, or, more commonly, you may just find a pile of feathers indicating that a hawk has made a catch.

Larger hawks, such as Red-shouldered, Red-tailed, and Broad-winged Hawks, that feed on small mammals may also be attracted to your feeder. These hawks are most likely drawn by the squirrels and chipmunks that are almost always present under a sunflower seed feeder if your yard is at all wooded.

In either case, the best plan of action is to enjoy getting an occasional good look at one of these hawks. In the case of the bird eaters, we may wish that they would go elsewhere, while in the case of the squirrel and mice hunters, we may wish them luck. But both are an important part of our avifauna, and they must eat too. Remember that all of our hawks are protected by state and federal laws and should not be harassed or harmed.

House Sparrow

House Sparrows are another European emigrant, having been introduced into this country in New York City's Central Park in the 1850s. They have spread across the continent and are now common birds

around rural farmsteads, especially where grain is stored or where there is livestock. In cities, they seem to aggregate around fast-food restaurants, at least here in the Carolinas.

The problem with House Sparrows is that they compete with native birds, especially Eastern Bluebirds, for nest boxes. House Sparrows build bulky nests, sometimes in the open but often behind billboards, in barn lofts, and in bluebird and Purple Martin houses. They can be very aggressive in the takeover and defense of birdhouses and usually win when there is competition. They are more difficult to keep out of bluebird houses than European Starlings because their smaller size allows them entry through the typical one-and-a-half-inch opening.

House Sparrows are not considered migratory birds and are not protected by federal or state laws. Be aware, however, that local laws on nonnative bird species are not uniform. In some areas all wildlife, whether native or not, is protected and cannot be harassed or harmed.

Mute Swans

Mute Swans are one of the largest species of waterfowl. They are native to Europe and were introduced into the United States in the late 1800s. They are often kept as domestic birds on park and estate ponds and lakes. They have escaped captivity many times, and feral populations have become established in several states, including both Carolinas. Mute Swans in this country are generally not migratory and remain in their chosen habitats all year.

There are several problems with Mute Swans. They are large, aggressive birds and are known to disrupt native nesting birds. When nesting in areas frequented by people, they may attack those who venture too

close to their nests. This may be particularly dangerous to small children.

There is also evidence from other states that they may compete with native Tundra Swans during the winter. In several states the feral population of Mute Swans has grown to such an extent that wildlife agencies are considering, or already employing, measures designed to reduce the population.

Woodpeckers

Woodpeckers are native species that are an important component of our avifauna. They are attractive, active birds, and several species will come regularly to suet feeders and even feeders filled with sunflower seeds.

We enjoy having them around, but there are at least two situations where they can be annoying or even destructive.

Male woodpeckers can be annoying when they use a wall or chimney of your house as a resonating chamber for a drum roll. While woodpeckers have a variety of calls, they often use their bill to peck on resonating surfaces, such as hollow trees, to establish and defend territory, as most other birds do with song. When they choose to do a long drum roll on your attic wall or chimney at daylight, it can make sleeping impossible. In this case, the racket will likely cease when the nesting season is over, and usually no damage is done to the house. You may also be able to discourage the bird with a fake snake or owl placed near the drumming site.

When woodpeckers are destructive, the situation is more difficult. If carpenter bees get into your wooden siding or the fascia boards on your house, they drill long tunnels where they lay their eggs and where the larvae live. If woodpeckers find the bee colony, they may decide to excavate the boards to get at the larvae. This exposes the damage done by the bees and leads to an unsightly mess—but the bees actually did most of the damage; the woodpeckers just uncovered it. The solution here is to get rid of the carpenter bees. An appropriate insecticide injected into the tunnels may kill the bees, but if the woodpeckers found them before you did, you may have carpentry work to do.

Remember that all of our woodpeckers are protected as migratory birds and may not be harassed or harmed.

Other Critters

It's natural for some predators to prey on birds. However, we may inadvertently assist predators when we attract birds to our property, leading to a concentration of birds that wouldn't otherwise exist. Here are a few of the most common predators that prey on birds, as well as some critters that can become nuisances around feeders and birdhouses.

House Cats

House cats are highly efficient predators of small birds. If you love both birds and cats, then be sure to keep your cats indoors as much as possible. You should also encourage local programs designed to reduce the numbers of feral cats in your community.

It's important not to place your feeders and birdbaths in locations just a few feet from dense cover where cats and other mammalian predators can hide and dart out to catch your birds. At the same time, it's also important to place both feeders and birdbaths in locations with es-

cape within a few yards, so birds can dive into cover if an avian predator appears.

Fire Ants

Fire ants are a major problem for ground-nesting birds in the southern United States. They attack the nests of birds such as the bobwhite and eat both eggs and small chicks. They are also known to climb into the nests of small birds in low, open areas and into birdhouses and eat the eggs and chicks.

Fire ants occur in all counties in South Carolina and in all of the eastern counties and a few mountain counties in North Carolina. They are continuing to spread and will likely soon be found in all of North Carolina. The complete elimination of fire ants is not possible at this time, but control is possible at the very local level. If you have a farm, control will require lots of effort and expense, and the effort must be on-going because fire ants will return to repopulate areas. In small areas, such as around the base of an Eastern Bluebird nest box, you can eliminate fire ants with insecticides or poison baits. Research on the best methods and materials for fire ant control is ongoing; see the websites of Extension Services at Clemson University or North Carolina State University for current detailed recommendations.

Snakes

The primary problem with snakes is that several species are excellent climbers and will readily climb most birdhouse support poles. Once in-

side a birdhouse, they may eat the eggs, nestlings, and even the adult birds. The solution is to place predator guards on the support posts.

Squirrels

Red, gray, and flying squirrels can be nuisances at bird feeders. They will actively compete for seeds (especially sunflower seeds) and suet put out for birds.

Squirrels will also enlarge the entrance holes of birdhouses if metal plates are not installed around them and will usurp the houses. Flying squirrels don't even need to enlarge the openings—they are small enough to enter the one-and-a-half-inch holes of bluebird houses.

The best solution to prevent squirrels from taking over boxes is to install predator guards, which prevent gray and red squirrels from reaching the boxes. To keep out flying squirrels, place the boxes well away from trees so that the squirrels cannot glide down to the boxes.

LEFT
A gray squirrel

ABOVE
A southern flying squirrel

Snow Geese
landing in a
cut cornfield

A Broader Perspective

While we often make direct efforts to attract birds to our living spaces, we also unintentionally interact with them in many ways—some positive and some negative. Any time that we modify the natural habitats around us, we affect the lives of the birds living there. When we clear-cut a section of forest, we remove the habitat for birds living there, but at the same time, when new growth begins, it becomes habitat for different species. When we clear land to build our communities, we make it impossible for most species to continue occupying the habitat, but we also create new possibilities for some species.

Human activities, especially around agriculture, inevitably create opportunities for some birds. For example, when corn is cut in late August and September in the Carolinas, Mourning Doves, Red-winged Blackbirds, Brown-headed Cowbirds, and grackles flock to the fields to feed on the waste grain. When soybeans are harvested later in the fall, Tundra Swans and Canada Geese find the waste beans an important food source. Winter wheat that's planted near refuges where Tundra Swans winter may become a food source for these birds. At the same time, the heavy use of chemicals in modern agriculture is likely having many negative effects on birds that use agricultural lands and may offset some of the positive effects of abundant waste grain. We need to better understand the broad and complicated relationship between birds and agriculture in order to minimize potential damage.

There are many such incidental ways that we affect the lives of birds. We must recognize that we have a major impact on the lives of birds and other animals that share the Carolinas with us humans. It is especially important that we understand how we affect species whose numbers are declining. It is sometimes possible to minimize or even eliminate negative impacts if we understand what is happening. With education and effort, we can do much to assure the continued presence of a diverse avifauna sharing our living spaces and in doing so enhancing our lives.

Currently several organizations are encouraging the use of native plants in our landscapes, which is a great idea for providing more natural foods for birds. The concept of leaving more of our urban landscapes in natural vegetation is also gaining strength, and this will provide more and better living spaces for birds.

We encourage you to continue your efforts to attract birds to your living spaces large and small and to support organizations such as the Audubon Society, wildlife federations, local land trusts, local garden clubs, and others that are working to ensure that we have healthy bird populations throughout the Carolinas.

Acknowledgments

The authors appreciate the help of the many people and organizations that have, both directly and indirectly, influenced and aided our efforts to produce this book. Thank you to all the folks who allowed us to use their properties as examples of the ways that we attract birds in the Carolinas. Thanks also to Chris Alexander, Josh Arrants, Lyne Askins, Kay McCutcheon, Eric Bolen, John Cely, Eddie Drayton, Walker Golder, Tee Lucas, Marcus Simpson, and Curtis Smalling for their input into this effort. Thanks to the folks at UNC Press for their availability, guidance, and assistance throughout this project. Special thanks to Erin Granville for her insightful suggestions, corrections, and guidance in the editing of the final manuscript.

For Further Reading

Carter, Robin M. *Finding Birds in South Carolina*. Columbia:
University of South Carolina Press, 1993.

Dobson, Clive. *Feeding Wild Birds in Winter*.
Willowdale, Ontario: Firefly Books, 1981.

Everett, Roger S. *Birds of Coastal South Carolina*.
Atglen, Pa.: Schiffer Publishing, 2007.

Fussell, J. O., III. *A Birder's Guide to Coastal North Carolina*.
Chapel Hill: University of North Carolina Press, 1994.

Gill, Frank B. *Ornithology*. 2nd ed. New York: W. H. Freeman, 1995.

Kress, Stephen W. *The Audubon Society Guide to Attracting
Birds*. New York: Charles Scribner's Sons, 1985.

Mizejewski, David. *Attracting Birds, Butterflies, and Other
Backyard Wildlife*. 2nd ed. Creative Homeowner, 2019.

Potter, Eloise, James Parnell, Robert Teulings, and Ricky
Davis. *Birds of the Carolinas*. 2nd ed. Chapel Hill:
University of North Carolina Press, 2007.

Simpson, Marcus. *Birds of the Blue Ridge Mountains*. Chapel
Hill: University of North Carolina Press, 1992.

Sprunt, Alexander, Jr., and E. B. Chamberlain. *South Carolina Bird Life*.
2nd ed. Columbia: University of South Carolina Press, 1970.

Swick, Nate. *American Birding Association Field Guide to Birds
of the Carolinas*. New York: Scott and Nix, 2016.

Thompson, Bill, III. *Southern Birds Backyard Guide*.
Birmingham, Ala.: Sweet Water Press, 2013.

Wray, David L., and H. T. Davis. *Birds of North Carolina*.
Rev. ed. Raleigh, N.C.: Bynum Printing Company.

Selected Websites

Acopian BirdSavers, www.birdsavers.com

American Bird Conservancy, www.abcbirds.org

Birds of North Carolina, http://ncbirds.carolinabirdclub.org

Bringing Nature Home, www.bringingnaturehome.net

Carolina Bird Club, www.carolinabirdclub.org

Carolina Nature, www.carolinanature.com

Carolina Raptor Center, www.carolinaraptorcenter.org

Clemson University, www.clemson.edu

Conserve Wildlife Foundation of New Jersey,
    www.conservewildlifenj.org

Cornell Laboratory of Ornithology, www.birds.cornell.edu

Golden-Winged Warbler Working Group, www.gwwa.org

National Audubon Society, www.audubon.org

National Audubon Society, North Carolina, nc.audubon.org

National Audubon Society, South Carolina, sc.audubon.org

National Wildlife Federation, www.nwf.org

North Carolina State University, https://content.ces.ncsu.edu
    /managing-backyards-and-other-urban-habitats-for-birds

North Carolina Wildlife Federation, www.ncwf.org

North Carolina Wildlife Resources Commission, www.ncwildlife.org

South Carolina Department of Natural Resources, www.dnr.sc.gov

South Carolina Wildlife Federation, www.scwf.org

Appendix: Ordinances on Bird Sanctuaries

A sign at the entrance to Boiling Springs Lake, North Carolina

North Carolina General Statutes Chapter 160A, Cities and Towns § 160A-188, Bird Sanctuaries

A city may by ordinance create and establish a bird sanctuary within the city limits. The ordinance may not protect any birds classed as a pest under Article 22A of Chapter 113 of the General Statutes and the Structural Pest Control Act of North Carolina of 1955 or the North Carolina Pesticide Law of 1971. When a bird sanctuary has been established, it shall be unlawful for any person to hunt, kill, trap, or otherwise take any protected birds within the city limits except pursuant to a permit issued by the North Carolina Wildlife Resources Commission under G.S. 113-274(c) (1a) or under any other license or permit of the Wildlife Resources Commission specifically made valid for use in taking birds within city limits.

South Carolina, Section 50-11-860, Department to Designate and Establish Sanctuaries; Agreements with Landowners

The department, without any costs whatsoever to the State, shall designate and establish sanctuaries where game, birds, and animals may breed unmolested, if any landowner enters into an agreement with the department to set aside and turn over to the State for that purpose a certain number of acres of land. There may be no hunting or trespassing upon these lands so designated as a sanctuary by anyone for five years from the date of the agreement. The department may post those lands so designated as a sanctuary in the name of the State and prosecute any persons hunting or trespassing on the lands. Any agreement entered into under authority given in this section may be terminated at any time by the landowner and the department.

Index